BRIGHTON AND HOVE ALBION F.C.
An A–Z

Dean Hayes

DEDICATION

To Brighton and Hove Albion fans everywhere

First published in 2002 by S. B. Publications,
19 Grove Road, Seaford, East Sussex BN25 1TP
Tel: 01323 893498

ISBN 1 85770 257 3

Designed and typeset by CGB, Lewes. Tel: 01273 476622
Printed by MFP Design & Print, Manchester
www.mfpprint.co.uk

ABOUT THE AUTHOR

Dean Hayes is an experienced freelance sports writer specialising in football and cricket. He was educated at Hayward Grammar School, Bolton, and West Midlands College of Physical Education, and was a Primary School Head Teacher until taking up writing on a permanent basis seven years ago.

He has played football in the Lancashire Amateur League, but he now concentrates solely on playing the summer game. This former cricket professional, now residing in the sunny climes of Pembrokeshire where he plays league cricket for Burton, has taken well over 2,000 wickets in league cricket.

Dean is married to Elaine and has one son and two stepchildren. This is his fifty-sixth book on football and his seventy-first overall.

Front cover: Bobby Zamora in action. *Photo: Sussex Express*
Back cover. Albion's last walk out onto the Goldstone Ground. *Photo: Nick Buckwell.*

ACKNOWLEDGEMENTS

The author wishes to thank the following for their invaluable assistance in producing this book:
Brighton and Hove Albion Football Club; The Association of Statisticians; The Football League Limited and The National Newspaper Library at Colindale.

Thanks also to the following individuals: Chris Horlock and Ben Hayes.

PICTURE CREDITS

Illustrations were kindly supplied by the *Lancashire Evening Post,* Chris Horlock, the *Sussex Express* and Nick Buckwell and they are individually credited. Others are from the author's own collection.

A

ABANDONED MATCHES

A match may be called off by the referee when it is in progress because conditions do not permit it to be completed. Generally speaking, far fewer matches are now abandoned because, if there is some doubt about playing the full game, it is more likely to be postponed.

The full list of Brighton's abandoned matches is as follows:

Date	Opponents	Competition	Score	Reason
02.10.1905	New Brompton	United League	1-0	Bad light (80 mins)
11.11.1907	Q.P.R.	Western League	1-0	Fog (25 mins)
16.01.1908	P.N.E.	FA Cup	2-1	Bad light (112mins)
18.01.1908	Southampton	Southern League	0-0	Fog (9 mins)
16.09.1968	Orient	Division Three	1-1	Muddy pitch (45mins)
01.01.1977	Swindon Town	Division Three	0-4	Waterlogged (67 mins)
27.04.1996	York City	Division Two	0-0	Pitch invasion (102mins)

ADAMS, MICKY

Micky Adams.
Photo: Lancashire Evening Post.

Micky Adams started his footballing career as an apprentice with Gillingham, winning England youth honours and appearing in 92 games for the Kent club before his transfer to Coventry City in the summer of 1983. A virtual ever-present in his three seasons at Highfield Road, he joined Leeds United before moving to Southampton. In five years at the Dell, he clocked up 174 first team appearances. After being given a free transfer, he had a brief spell at Stoke City before joining Fulham as player-coach.

In February 1996 he was appointed the club's player-manager, at the time the youngest

5

in the league. He led the club to promotion to the Second Division in his first season in charge. In October 1997 he was allowed to leave Craven Cottage and had brief spells in charge of Swansea and Brentford before becoming assistant-manager at Nottingham Forest.

In April 1999, Adams took over the reins at Brighton, the Seagulls winning their first match under his managership 1-0 against Shrewsbury Town. In his first full season the club finished in mid-table but in 2000-01, he led the Seagulls to the Third Division Championship. He then left to become assistant-manager to Dave Bassett at Leicester City and has now been appointed the Foxes' manager for the forthcoming season.

ADDINALL, BERT

Bert Addinall played his early football for Queen's Park Rangers during the latter years of the Second World War and signed official forms in the 1946 close season. He soon broke into the Rangers' first team and from 1948 to 1952 – the four seasons that the Loftus Road club spent in the Second Division – he was the leading scorer. As a centre-forward he was typical of the era , being fairly aggressive and always committed to scoring goals. He netted 74 times in 172 games before leaving Rangers for Brighton midway through the 1952-53 season.

Addinall made a goal-scoring debut for Albion in a 2-1 win at Torquay United. Although he only played in nineteen games, he was joint top scorer with Ken Bennett with 11 goals. The following season, Albion were runners-up to Ipswich town in the Third Division (South) with Addinall heading the club's charts with 20 goals, including scoring in six consecutive league games midway through the campaign. He had scored 33 goals in 63 League and Cup games when, in the close season, he was surprisingly allowed to join Crystal Palace where he finished his first-class career.

AGGREGATE SCORE

Brighton's highest aggregate score in any competition came in the Football League Cup second round tie against Bradford City in 1985-86. In the first leg at the Goldstone Ground, Danny Wilson netted a hat-trick in a 5-2 win for the Seagulls. In the second leg, played at the Odsal

Stadium, home of Rugby League giants Bradford Northern, goals from Biley and Ferguson gave Brighton a 2-0 win and an aggregate victory of 7-2.

APPEARANCES

Ernie Wilson holds the record for the highest number of League and Cup appearances in a Brighton and Hove Albion shirt with a total of 566 games to his credit between 1922 and 1936. The players with the highest number of appearances are as follows:

	League	FA Cup	FLg Cup	Others	Total
Ernie Wilson	509	49	-	8	566
Peter O'Sullivan	432(3)	25	31	-	488(3)
Norman Gall	427(13)	26(1)	21	-	474(14)
Glen Wilson	409	27	-	-	436
Bobby Farrell	382	38	-	10	430
Des Tennant	400	24	-	-	424
Reg Wilkinson	361	30	-	5	396
Brian Powney	351	20	15	-	386
Steve Gatting	316(3)	26	14	10	366(3)
Dave Walker	310	27	-	12	349

ATTENDANCE – AVERAGE

Brighton's average home league attendances for the past ten seasons have been as follows:

1992-93	6,710	1997-98	2,329
1993-94	7,730	1998-99	3,253
1994-95	7,563	1999-00	5,733
1995-96	5,448	2000-01	6,603
1996-97	5,844	2001-02	6,585

ATTENDANCE – HIGHEST

The record attendance at the Goldstone Ground is 36,747 for the Second Division game with Fulham on 27 December 1958. The match ended in a 3-0 win for the Seagulls with Tommy Dixon scoring twice and Adrian Thorne netting the club's other goal.

ATTENDANCE – LOWEST

The lowest attendance at the Goldstone Ground is 1,607 for the visit of Bournemouth in an Autoglass Trophy group game on 9 December 1992. For the record, the Seagulls won 3-2 with goals from Wilkinson, Walker and Nogan.

ATTWOOD, ARTHUR

Arthur Attwood joined Brighton from Bristol Rovers midway through the 1931-32 season and although he failed to score on his debut in a 3-2  defeat at the hands of Fulham, he went on to score 25 goals in 27 games. In fact, Attwood scored in each of his next eight games – his total of 14 goals including a hat-trick in a 4-0 win over Coventry City. Before the season was out, he had netted another treble in a 4-1 defeat of Thames and four goals in a 7-0 rout of Gillingham.

The following season, Attwood netted six of Brighton's goals in a 12-0 demolition of non-League Shoreham in an FA Cup first qualifying round match. He went on to score 35 League and Cup goals (including the qualifying competition) netting a hat-trick on the final day of the season as

Arthur Attwood.

Bristol City were beaten 7-0.

Attwood had made a good start to the 1933-34 campaign when he was struck down by appendicitis and forced to miss the second half of the season. He did not return to the side until the latter stages of the following campaign before leaving the club in the close season. One of Brighton's most prolific strikers, he had netted 75 goals in 104 first team games.

AUTOGLASS TROPHY

The Autoglass Trophy replaced the Leyland Daf Cup for the 1991-92 season but it was the following campaign, after their relegation, that the

Seagulls first took part in the competition. In their group games, Albion drew 1-1 at Reading and beat Bournemouth 3-2 at the Goldstone Ground to qualify for the knockout stages with Darren Wilkinson scoring in both games. They needed extra time to run out winners 4-2 over Walsall and set up a southern area quarter-final meeting with Exeter City.

Disappointingly only 1,875 turned up to cheer on the Seagulls who were below par and lost 1-0 to the Grecians. In 1993-94, Albion lost 4-1 at Fulham and then were held at home 2-2 by Reading – results that prevented them qualifying for the knockout stages.

AUTOWINDSCREEN SHIELD

This competition replaced the Autoglass Trophy in the 1994-95 season, and the Seagulls drew their first match 1-1 at Gillingham, with Junior McDougald scoring the Brighton goal, but then lost 1-0 at home to Brentford and so failed to qualify for the knockout stages.

In 1995-96, two goals by on-loan Gary Bell helped them beat Cambridge United 4-1 at the Abbey Stadium and although they lost 2-0 at Bristol Rovers in their other group match they had done enough to qualify for the knockout stages. A late Denny Mundee penalty gave Albion a 2-1 win at Walsall and a place in the southern area quarter-final. Despite putting up a brave fight, they went down 4-2 at Shrewsbury Town.

In 1996-97, the competition was switched to a straight knockout. Brighton's first round opponents were Fulham and at the end of 90 minutes the teams were level at 2-2. The game went into extra time with the golden goal rule applying. Albion full-back James Virgo netted the sudden death decider. In the second round Brighton lost 1-0 to Plymouth.

In 1997-98, Albion crashed out of the competition at the first hurdle, suffering their heaviest defeat in losing 5-0 at Walsall. The next season was no better as they were beaten 5-1 at home by Millwall, after initially taking the lead. In 1999-2000, a last minute Gary Hart goal gave them revenge over Millwall and a trip to Bournemouth in round two. Neither team could score within normal time and the game went into sudden death. It was the Cherries' James Hayter who netted after 102 minutes to win the game for the home side.

AWAY MATCHES

Brighton and Hove Albion's best away win came in the Football League on 1 February 1930 when they won 8-2 at Merthyr Town, a match in which Dan Kirkwood scored four of the goals.

The Seagulls' worst defeat away from home was 9-0 by Middlesbrough on 23 August 1958. The club have also conceded eight goals on their travels when they lost 8-0 at Northampton Town on 1 November 1966 in a fourth round League Cup replay.

AWAY SEASONS

The club's highest number of away wins came in 1971-72 when they won 12 of their 23 matches in finishing runners-up to Aston Villa in the Third Division.

The Seagulls won just one away game in the 1972-73 and the 1982-83 seaons when they finished bottom of Division's Two and One respectively.

B

BAILEY, MIKE

Mike Bailey played his early football with non-League Gorleston before joining Charlton Athletic. His performances for the Addicks led to him winning full international honours for England, as he developed into one of the best wing-halves in the country. Bailey, who was also Charlton's captain, broke a leg but recovered to play in 169 games before joining Wolverhampton Wanderers.

He helped the Molineux club win promotion to the First Division in 1966-67 and skippered the side to victory over Manchester City in the League Cup Final of 1974. On leaving Wolves after scoring 25 goals in 436 games, he played for Minnesota Kicks in the NASL before becoming player-coach of Hereford United and then manager of Charlton Athletic. He led the club to promotion to the Second Division before being appointed manager of Brighton in the summer of 1981.

In his first season at the Goldstone Ground, he led the Seagulls to thirteenth place in the First Division but a poor start the following season saw Bailey part company with the south coast club.

BAXTER, BOBBY

Bobby Baxter began his Football League career with Darlington where he had scored a goal every other game but on his arrival at the Goldstone Ground in the summer of 1961, he was converted to full-back. He made his Albion debut wearing the No.6 shirt in a goalless home draw against Preston North End and wore Nos. 10 and 11 before settling into the left-back spot.

Although Albion were relegated at the end of Baxter's first season with the club, he had not let anyone down and started the following campaign as first-choice No.3. Unfortunately the Seagulls suffered a second successive relegation and in 1963-64 he was forced to miss

much of the action through injury. He was back to full fitness the following season, playing his part in the club winning the Fourth Division Championship. He continued to impress over the next two seasons, taking his total of appearances, in which he scored seven goals, to 220 before leaving to play for Torquay United.

After two seasons at Plainmoor, his career turned full circle when he returned to the north-east to end his league football-playing days with his first club, Darlington.

BEAMISH, KEN

Much-travelled striker Ken Beamish began his Football League career with Tranmere Rovers, making his debut at Chesterfield in April 1966. However, it was the latter end of 1967-68 before he established himself as a regular in the Tranmere side. The following season he topped the club's scoring charts and netted a hat-trick in a 6-2 defeat of Oldham Athletic. Beamish continued to top Rovers' scoring charts for the next four seasons before leaving Prenton Park to join Brighton as the Seagulls made their final push for promotion from Division Three.

Brighton paid a then club record fee of £25,000 for Beamish's services but it was money well spent as his six goals in 12 starts helped them achieve their promotion. In 1972-73 he was joint top scorer with nine goals as Brighton finished bottom of the Second Division to make an immediate return. The following season, Beamish was the leading scorer with 12 goals as he and Barry Bridges netted a number of vital goals to prevent the club going straight down to the Fourth Division. He had scored 28 goals in 99 games when he left the Goldstone Ground to join Blackburn Rovers.

In his first season at Ewood Park he helped Blackburn win the Third Division Championship, but after finding goals harder to come by in the higher grade of football he moved to Port Vale. He later played for Bury before returning to play for Tranmere Rovers. He had scored 81 goals in

278 games in his two spells with the Wirral-based club before moving to Swindon Town as the club's player-coach. In March 1983 he was appointed manager of the County Ground club before returning to Blackburn as the club's commercial manager.

BENNETT, KEN

Unable to make the grade with Tottenham Hotspur, Ken Bennett joined Southend United and later played for Bournemouth before drifting into non-League football with Guildford City. Brighton gave him another chance at League level and the inside-forward made his League debut in a 2-2 home draw against Torquay United on the opening day of the 1950-51 season, winning a regular place in the Albion side midway through the campaign.

In 1951-52, Bennett was the club's leading scorer with 18 goals as Albion finished fifth in the Third Division (South). He continued to score on a regular basis the following season, hitting three doubles in the space of six games. During the close season, Ken Bennett, who had scored 41 goals in 107 games, went to Crystal Palace in a direct swap for his namesake Ron Bennett. He spent just one season at Selhurst Park before hanging up his boots.

BERTOLINI, JACK

Alloa-born wing-half Jack Bertolini began his career in the Scottish League with Stirling Albion before coming south of the border to play for Workington. He had scored 35 goals in 181 League games for the Cumbrian outfit when, in July 1958, Brighton manager Billy Lane brought him to the Goldstone Ground.

Bertolini had a disastrous debut as a member of the Brighton side beaten 9-0 at Middlesbrough on the opening day of the 1958-59 season. Despite that heavy defeat, Albion recovered and Bertolini played his part in helping the club end the season in mid-table. An ever-present for the next four seasons, Bertolini played in 204 consecutive League games before injury forced him to miss the game against Bradford Park Avenue in September 1963. Injuries then began to restrict his number of first team appearances and Jack Bertolini, who had scored 14 quite often vital goals in 279 games, was forced to retire somewhat prematurely.

BEST STARTS

Brighton and Hove Albion were unbeaten for the first eight League games of both the 1953-54 and 1977-78 seasons.

In 1953-54, the Seagulls won seven and drew one of their matches before losing 2-0 at Southend United on 15 September 1953. The club ended the season as runners-up in the Third Division (South).

In 1977-78, when the club finished fourth in Division Two, they were once again undefeated in their opening eight League games until losing 4-3 at Charlton Athletic on 4 October 1977.

BOOTH, BILLY

Wing-half Billy Booth played his early football for Sheffield United before joining Brighton in the summer of 1908. One of a number of new signings, he made his Albion debut in a 3-1 home defeat by Southampton on the opening day of the 1908-09 season. Booth was ever-present the following term as Brighton won the Southern League Championship but failed to get on the scoresheet.

Billy Booth

He was a member of the Albion side that won the FA Charity Shield and was again ever-present in 1910-11, scoring his first goal for the club in a 2-1 defeat at Exeter City. He continued to shine for Albion and midway through the 1912-13 season was chosen as England's reserve for the match with Ireland in Belfast and for the Southern League against the Irish League at The Den.

The following season was Billy Booth's benefit season, when he was again ever-present and made a number of appearances in the Southern League representative side. He returned to the Goldstone Ground after the hostilities and took his total of appearances in which he scored nine goals to 369. He then left the club before the start of their inaugural season of League football.

BRADY, LIAM

The play-maker of Arsenal's highly successful teams of the 1970s, Liam Brady was one of the great crowd pleasers in the Gunners' side. He was a member of Arsenal's 1979 FA Cup winning team against Manchester United and picked up a loser's medal in the 1978 and 1980 Cup Finals against Ipswich Town and West Ham United. He crowned an outstanding Arsenal career by steering the club to the European Cup Winners' Cup Final in 1980 but his last appearance for the Gunners was marred by defeat. Locked at 0-0 with Valencia after extra-time, Arsenal lost the penalty shoot-out 5-4.

Brady's glittering career took him to Juventus, Sampdoria, Internazionale and Ascoli before he made a welcome return to the Football League with West Ham United in 1986-87. He launched an outstanding career for the Republic of Ireland in 1975 and was still in the squad when Jack Charlton led them to the European Championships in the summer of 1988. He later managed Celtic before taking over the reins at the Goldstone Ground in December 1993, as the Seagulls' new chairman Greg Stanley staved off another High Court action by increasing his stake in the club and settling various tax debts. Sadly, in his two seasons, the club could finish no higher than mid-table in the Second Division and midway through 1995-96 he resigned.

BREMNER, KEVIN

The younger brother of Scottish international Des Bremner, the lightweight striker began his career with Colchester United. His early performances were impressive but towards the end of his stay at Layer Road, he set something of a record. In 1982-83 he played for five different clubs and scored for each of them. He had scored at a rate of a goal every other game for Colchester and did the same at his next two clubs, Reading and Millwall, before joining Brighton in July 1987.

Bremner made his debut in the 1-0 home win over York City on the opening day of the 1987-88 season. He had scored 11 goals in his first 24 games but then went almost six months without finding the net in League games. Yet he kept his place in the side, helping the club win promotion to Division Two as runners-up to Sunderland.

In 1988-89 he was much more consistent in front of goal, netting 15 times in 41 outings as he and Garry Nelson ended the season as joint top scorers in the League. Included in this total was his first hat-trick for the club as the Seagulls beat Birmingham City 4-0.

The following campaign, Bremner topped the club's scoring charts with 12 goals, taking his total to 40 in 141 games before moving on to Peterborough United. He later moved back north of the border to play for Dundee, and he did have a loan spell with Shrewsbury Town.

BRIGHTON AND HOVE RANGERS

Following the collapse of Brighton United, the players went their separate ways. North End Rangers were formed in 1891 and three years later won the Brighton Challenge Cup, followed in 1895 by winning the Sussex Junior Cup Final. In 1896 they became founder members of the East Sussex League, winning the Championship in its first season.

In 1898-99 the club hit hard times, but with the permission of the FA it was reorganised and its name changed to Brighton and Hove Rangers. Home games were played at Home Farm, Withdean and its inaugural match was played there in September 1900 against a strong Clapton side. It ended in a goalless draw. The club played a number of friendly matches and also reached the final of the Sussex Senior Cup, losing 3-1 to Eastbourne. In the final of the Brighton Challenge Shield the side went down 3-2 to Brighton Athletic.

BRIGHTON UNITED

After beating West Sussex Senior League side Southwick 8-1 in a friendly, the Brighton United opened their first season of Southern League football in 1898-99 with a visit to the reigning champions, Southampton. The Saints, with three internationals in their side, dominated the match and won 4-1. The club's form throughout that season, fluctuated and it ended the campaign in tenth place from thirteen teams.

In 1899-1900, the Greenbacks, so-called because of their green shirts and white shorts, failed to win a single away game and with attendances dwindling, the club was wound up with four league games still to be played.

BURTENSHAW, STEVE

Steve Burtenshaw served Brighton as a wing-half for fourteen seasons, making the first of his 252 League and Cup appearances in a 5-1 win at Exeter City in April 1953. Midway through the following season, when he had established himself in the Albion side, he was called up for National Service. He did not play again until 1956-57 when he helped Brighton finish sixth in the Third Division (South). The following season he was an important member of the side that won that section's Championship, although injuries restricted his appearances towards the end of the campaign.

He scored his first goal for the club in the fifth game of the 1958-59 season as Albion won their first game in Division Two, beating Grimsby Town 2-0. After a season decimated with injuries, Burtenshaw missed very few matches and was ever-present in 1961-62 when the club finished bottom of the Second Division. Although Albion suffered a second successive relegation in 1962-63 Burtenshaw had a fine season. However, when Albion won the Fourth Division Championship in 1964-65, he only made two appearances.

By now he had been encouraged to take up coaching by Brighton boss George Curtis, and when he retired he secured a job with Arsenal as reserve team coach. After a short spell coaching Queen's Park Rangers, he moved into management with Sheffield Wednesday.

He found victories hard to come by and after a poor start to the 1975-76 season, his contract was terminated. He then had a spell as manager of Queen's Park Rangers but that too ended in disaster as the Loftus Road club were relegated at the end of his first season.

BYRNE, JOHN

Republic of Ireland international John Byrne began his career with York City before joining Queen's Park Rangers. He was a member of the side that lost to Oxford United in the 1986 League Cup Final but two years later was transferred to French club, Le Havre, for £175,000.

John Byrne.
Photo: Lancashire Evening Post.

On his return to these shores in the summer of 1990, he joined Brighton, making his debut as a substitute for Mark Barham in a 3-2 win over Charlton Athletic. He gained a place in the starting line-up and scored five goals in his first eight outings, going on to help the Seagulls finish in the play-offs.

During the early part of the 1991-92 season, Byrne left to join Sunderland for a fee of £225,000 but he returned to the Goldstone ground on loan after a spell with Millwall towards the end of the following campaign. He scored twice on the final day in a 3-2 win over Chester that saw Albion finish three points outside the play-offs.

After a couple of seasons with Oxford United, Byrne joined the Seagulls for a third spell, taking his tally of goals to 22 in 97 appearances.

C

CAPACITY

The capacity of the Withdean Stadium in 2001-02 was 6,960.

CAPTAINS

One of the earliest captains was Joe Leeming who joined Albion from Bury in the summer of 1908. He led the club to the Southern League Championship in 1909-10 when, as a popular full-back, he was ever-present. He also captained Albion to victory over First Division Aston Villa in the FA Charity Shield.

Jack Rutherford, a former Luton Town centre-half, was named as club captain for Brighton's first season of League football but he was absent for the inaugural match against Southend United, the skipper being Jack Woodhouse.

When Brighton won the Third Division (South) Championship in 1957-58, they were led by long-serving Glen Wilson. He missed only one game that season and scored from the spot in the 6-0 defeat of Watford on the final day of the campaign.

Jimmy Collins joined Albion from Tottenham Hotspur, where he had spent much of his career in the White Hart Lane club's reserve side. He was hugely popular with the Goldstone faithful and led the club to the Fourth Division Championship in 1964-65.

When Albion won promotion to the Second Division in 1971-72, they were led by former Bolton and Northern Ireland international centre-half John Napier.

Brian Horton skippered Albion to two promotions. In 1976-77 he was the driving force behind the club winning promotion to Division Two and two seasons later top-scored in the League with 11 goals as Albion made it to the top flight.

When Albion reached the FA Cup Final in 1983, Steve Foster was the club captain but he was suspended for the final and the side was skippered by Tony Grealish to a 2-2 draw. Foster returned to lead the Seagulls in the replay, which they lost 4-0.

Former Chelsea defender, Doug Rougvie, spent just one season at the Goldstone Ground and captained the club to promotion to Division Two.

When Albion won the Third Division title in 2000-01, they were captained by Paul Rogers, a virtual ever-present in the side. Last season, when they won their second successive Championship, they were led by Danny Cullip.

CASE, JIMMY

Jimmy Case played non-League football for South Liverpool before going to Anfield in May 1973. In the next eight years, he made well over 200 League and Cup appearances, scoring 45 goals. He had a ferocious shot that produced a number of spectacular goals, including the equaliser against Manchester United in the 1977 FA Cup Final. In his stay at Anfield, he won three European Cup medals, four League Championship medals and a UEFA Cup winners' medal.

Spectacular goal scorer, Jimmy Case, in action

Photo: Lancashire Evening Post.

During the summer of 1981 Case signed for Brighton in a £350,000 transfer deal and made his debut in a 1-1 draw at West Ham United on the opening day of the 1981-82 season. Although he only scored three goals in his first season with the Seagulls, one was against his former club in a 3-3 draw at the Goldstone Ground.

He could do little to prevent the club's relegation the following season but was instrumental in it reaching the FA Cup Final with goals in the fourth round (Manchester City Home 4-0) fifth round (Liverpool Away 2-1)

20

sixth round (Norwich City Home 1-0) and semi-final (Sheffield Wednesday at Highbury 2-1).

Case continued to be an important member of the Albion side for the next two seasons, going on to score 15 goals in 147 games – including a hat-trick in a 7-0 defeat of Charlton Athletic – before joining Southampton.

Over the next few seasons he showed he had lost none of his tenacity, playing in 264 games for the Saints before ending his playing career with spells at Bournemouth, Halifax and Wrexham.

In November 1995 he was appointed manager of Brighton but parted company with the club following its relegation to the Third Division.

CATTLIN, CHRIS

Chris Cattlin began his career with Huddersfield Town before joining Coventry City in March 1968 for a fee of £70,000, then a British record for a left-back. During eight seasons at Highfield Road, Cattlin won two caps for England at Under 23 level and was unlucky not to win full international honours. When he was given a free transfer at the end of the 1975-76 season, City supporters raised a petition in the hope of making the club have a change of heart. It was all to no avail and Cattlin joined Brighton and Hove Albion.

He played his first game for the Seagulls in a 1-1 draw at Southend on the opening day of the 1976-77 season, going on to help the club finish as runners-up to Mansfield Town and so win promotion to the Second Division. He scored his only League goal for the side against the Stags in a 1-1 draw at Field Mill.

Albion player, coach and manager, Chris Cattlin.
Photo: Lancashire Evening Post.

Cattlin had another outstanding season in 1977-78 as Albion reached

21

the top flight at the first attempt. He was still an important member of the Brighton side the following season when the team won promotion to the First Division as runners-up to Crystal Palace.

Unable to make the first team in the higher bracket, Cattlin had scored two goals in 114 League and Cup games when a persistent Achilles tendon injury forced his retirement. In July 1983, after three years out of the game, he was appointed as the club's first team coach and, before midway through the 1983-84 season, he replaced Jimmy Melia as manager. In his first season in charge, the Seagulls finished ninth in Division Two. However, maintaining mid-table position was not considered good enough and despite getting to the sixth round of the FA Cup he was sacked shortly afterwards.

Cattlin then launched a legal action, alleging wrongful dismissal, and the club countered with allegations of negligence and breach of duty. Three years later the matter was resolved by an out of court settlement in Cattlin's favour. He later ran a rock shop on the sea front at Brighton.

CENTURIES

Only one player has scored more than 100 League goals for the Seagulls and that is Tommy Cook with 114 strikes in his Brighton career (1921-1929). In all games, including wartime fixtures, Bert Stephens scored 174 goals and Jock Davie 120, and Cook's overall total was 123.

Eric Gill holds the club record for the most consecutive Football League appearances with 222. Other players to have made more than 100 consecutive appearances during their careers with Brighton are Jack Bertolini (204) Peter O'Sullivan (176) Billy Hayes (160) Gary Williams (129) and Dean Wilkins (106).

CHAMPIONSHIPS

Brighton and Hove Albion have won a divisional Championship on four occasions:

Third Division (South) 1957-58
Albion's form in the opening weeks of the campaign was outstanding – they won six and drew one of their first seven matches. In spite of a

sequence of four successive defeats, the Seagulls bounced back and an exciting title race developed. Alhough the club endured an indifferent Easter holiday programme – just three points from three games – it led the Division by a point from Plymouth Argyle, with a game in hand.

Because the season in those days had to finish in April, Albion had to play their last four games in eight days. After drawing at Port Vale, Dennis Foreman's last minute goal gave them victory at Watford. A point at fourth-placed Brentford would have given Brighton the title but the Bees won 1-0. A crowd of 31,038 turned up at the Goldstone Ground to see the last game of the season against Watford. Adrian Thorne netted a hat-trick in the space of four minutes and the Seagulls went on to win 6-0 and so clinch their first divisional Championship.

	P	W	L	D	F	A	Pts
Brighton and Hove Albion	46	24	12	10	88	64	60
Brentford	46	24	10	12	82	56	58
Plymouth Argyle	46	25	8	13	67	48	58

Fourth Division 1964-65

New signing Bobby Smith from Spurs scored twice on his debut in a 3-1 win over Barrow on the opening day of the season and, although Albion were unbeaten after five matches, three successive away defeats took them into mid-table. Four victories on the trot, including a 6-0 mauling of Notts County, lifted them back into the promotion pack. After the turn of the year, nine wins in eleven games kept Brighton in contention. There were just four games left – home and away clashes with re-election strugglers Stockport County and Darlington – but the promotion tussle was a close run affair with eight clubs still in with a chance. Maximum points were taken off Stockport but the Seagulls lost 2-0 at Darlington. A crowd of 31,423 turned out at the Goldstone Ground for the final game of the season against Darlington. Albion needed a point for promotion and two for the title. Goals from Collins, Smith and Gould helped Albion to a 3-1 win.

	P	W	D	L	F	A	Pts
Brighton and Hove Albion	46	26	11	9	102	57	63
Millwall	46	23	16	7	78	45	62
York City	46	28	6	12	91	56	62

Third Division 2000-01

After losing three of their first four fixtures, the Seagulls won seven and drew two of their next nine games with Bobby Zamora netting a hat-trick in a 6-2 defeat of Torquay United. Also during that unbeaten run, they kept six clean sheets. The Seagulls were never out of contention for a promotion place and with Zamora topping the Third Division scoring charts with 28 goals, they won the Championship, finishing ten points clear of runners-up Cardiff City.

	P	W	D	L	F	A	Pts
Brighton and Hove Albion	46	28	8	10	73	35	92
Cardiff City	46	23	13	10	95	58	82
Chesterfield	46	25	14	7	79	42	80*

*Nine points deducted for breach of rules

Second Division 2001-02

After a goalless draw at Cambridge United on the opening day of the season, Albion lost just one of their opening eleven fixtures before losing their only match at the Withdean Stadium 2-1 to Brentford. The Seagulls then won six and drew six of their next 12 league games. Undefeated in their last ten games of the season, Albion finished six points clear of the runners-up, Reading. Bobby Zamora was again the division's leading scorer with 28 goals.

	P	W	D	L	F	A	Pts
Brighton and Hove Albion	46	25	15	6	66	42	90
Reading	46	23	15	8	70	43	84
Brentford	46	24	11	11	77	43	83

CHAPMAN, IAN

Ian Chapman made his Albion debut in a 2-0 defeat at Birmingham City on 14 February 1987 when he was 16 years 259 days old – the youngest player to represent the club. With Brighton already relegated he returned to the side for the final four games of the season.

He did not appear at all the following season as the club won promotion to the Second Division but midway through 1988-89 he won a regular place in the side. The following season he missed only a handful of games and scored his first goal for the club in a 2-0 win at Bournemouth. He was a member of the side that reached the play-offs in 1990-91, and showed his versatility over the next few seasons by appearing in six different numbered outfield shirts before settling into the left-back berth.

Tenacious and committed, he scored 16 goals in 331 games for the Seagulls before being given a free transfer and joining Gillingham. He was a first team regular in his first season at the Priestfield Stadium but unfortunately a bad knee injury forced his retirement from first-class football.

CHARITY SHIELD

Today the Charity Shield is played as a curtain raiser to the new season with the Premier League champions playing the FA Cup holders. However there was a time, for a period of five years from 1908, when the champions of the Southern League and Football League met in the Charity Shield. So it was that on 5 September 1910, Brighton and Hove Albion met Aston Villa at Stamford Bridge. In a closely fought encounter, Charlie Webb scored the game's only goal to make Brighton the third winners of the FA Charity Shield behind Manchester United and Newcastle United.

CHIVERS, GARY

Chelsea were already condemned to relegation to the Second Division when Gary Chivers made his Football League debut in April 1979 but the following season he was a regular member of Geoff Hurst's promotion-chasing team. He was one of the best young defenders in the Second Division, playing alongside the centre-half, but then his form inexplicably slumped and he was not always sure of a place in the starting line-up.

After brief spells with Swansea City, Queen's Park Rangers and Watford, Chivers arrived at the Goldstone Ground on transfer deadline day in March 1988, making his debut in a goalless

Gary Chivers.
Photo: Lancashire Evening Post

25

home draw against Grimsby Town. He appeared in the last ten games of the season – seven of which were won and three drawn – as Albion won promotion to Division Two. An ever-present in 1988-89, he scored a number of vital goals that enabled the club to avoid an immediate return to the Third Division.

Chivers missed very few games over the next four seasons and helped the club reach the play-offs in 1990-91. He had scored 16 goals in 252 League and Cup games when, in November 1993, he moved to Bournemouth where he ended his first-class career.

CLEAN SHEETS

This is the expression used to describe a goalkeeper's performance when he does not concede a goal. In 1923-24, Billy Hayes kept 21 clean sheets in 42 League games as Brighton finished fifth in the Third Division (South). He also kept two clean sheets in that season's FA Cup competition.

In 2000-01, the Seagulls managed to keep 24 clean sheets when winning the Third Division Championship, but two goalkeepers, Michael Kuipers (18) and Mark Cartwright (6), played their part in the club achieving that feat.

CLOUGH, BRIAN

One of the game's greatest marksmen with 204 goals in 222 appearances for Middlesbrough before moving to Sunderland, Brian Clough was the leading scorer in the Second Division for three consecutive seasons and scored 40 goals or more every season from 1956 to 1960.

An injury received on Boxing Day 1962 virtually ended his playing career, and after a spell on Sunderland's coaching staff, he took his first steps in management with Hartlepool United. Joined by Peter Taylor, he turned the club's fortunes around, building a squad that was to be promoted in 1967-68. By then, however, Clough and Taylor had moved to Derby County, a side they at once led to the Second Division Championship. In 1971-72, the Rams won the League Championship and the following season reached the semi-finals of the European Cup.

In October 1973 Clough resigned as Derby manager following a dispute with the chairman, Sam Longson. The following month he and Taylor accepted an offer to manage Third Division Brighton. Clough did not take long to assert his authority and players came and went in quick succession. But Albion were beaten 8-2 at home by Bristol Rovers and 4-0 by non-League Walton and Hersham in the FA Cup.

Clough left the Goldstone Ground in July 1974 to take over at Leeds United but he was sacked after only 44 days in charge, and took over the reins at Nottingham Forest. In the next eighteen years he was to produce some golden moments for that club, including a League Championship, four League Cup wins and two European Cup successes. There is no doubt that Brian Clough was one of the greatest managers of all time. He retired in May 1993 amidst a lot of bad publicity, having won just about everything there was to win.

CODNER, ROBERT

Unable to make much headway with Leicester City, midfielder Robert Codner moved into non-League football with Barnet before the Seagulls gave the England semi-professional international another chance at League level in the summer of 1988. He played his first game in a 2-1 defeat at home to Bournemouth, but spent his first season with the club in and out of the side, only establishing himself as a first team regular in 1989-90 when he scored nine goals in 45 League games.

The following season he was instrumental in helping the Seagulls reach the play-offs, where they lost to Notts County in the final. Codner remained at the Goldstone Ground for a further four seasons, taking his total appearances, in which he scored 47 goals, to 315 before joining Reading.

His stay at Elm Park was brief as he was unable to impose himself in the Royals' midfield. After a trial with Peterborough United, he rejoined Barnet before ending his League career with Southend United.

COLLINS, JIMMY

Jimmy Collins joined Tottenham Hotspur after helping the Scottish junior Club, Lugar Boswell Thistle, win the Scottish Youth Cup. He was a regular goal scorer for the reserves but his only League appearances for the White Hart Lane club were as understudy for his fellow Scot, John White. With players such as White, Eddie Clayton and John Smith ahead of him in the pecking order, he was allowed to move to Brighton for a fee of £9,000.

After making his debut in a 1-0 defeat at Carlisle United, Collins played in the remaining 34 games of the 1962-63 season but could not prevent the Seagulls being relegated to the Fourth Division.

He was an ever-present in 1963-64 and contributed 12 goals in Brighton's brave attempt to win promotion at the first attempt. In 1964-65 he captained the side to the Fourth Division Championship, netting 17 goals in 45 games as Albion scored 102 goals during the course of the campaign. Collins was then moved into more of a defensive midfield role and spent two more seasons with Brighton, scoring 48 goals in 221 League and Cup games, before leaving to join non-League Wimbledon.

COLOURS

It was the influence of Brighton College which first stimulated regional interest, the school itself grooming several England internationals. Even the club's first colours of red, white and blue had all the appearance of contemporary school strips.

By the time the club achieved success in the Southern League, players were wearing blue and white stripes. The Seagulls had a great record in the Third Division (South) for more than thirty years without winning anything but in 1958 they gained promotion to the Second Division. After four years in that Division there followed consecutive drops to the Fourth Division. During this time the club sported blue shirts with white sleeves before returning to stripes.

During the heady days of First Division football and an appearance in the 1983 FA Cup Final, Brighton wore blue shirts with white trimmings. Since then, the early red has returned in trims, and styles have changed virtually every year.

The club's present colours are blue and white striped shirts, white shorts and blue stockings. The change strip is red and black striped shirts, black shorts and black stockings.

CONNOR, TERRY

Terry Connor was just 17 years old when he came on as a substitute to make his debut and netted the only goal of the game for Leeds United against West Bromwich Albion. He continued the happy knack of scoring early in his career with Leeds but then lost form in the struggling Leeds team.

In March 1983 he was traded for Brighton's Andy Ritchie and made his Seagulls' debut in a goal-less home draw against Aston Villa. His first goal for the Seagulls was the winner against Coventry City but sadly it was not enough to keep them in the top flight.

In 1983-84 Connor was the club's leading scorer with 17 goals and again the following season with 16. He formed a good strike partnership with Dean Saunders, scoring on a regular basis, but

Terry Connor in a struggle for possession.

Photo: Lancashire Evening Post.

although he headed the charts again in 1986-87, he could not prevent Albion finishing bottom of the Second Division. Connor, who had scored 59 goals in 174 games for Albion, left the club to return to top flight football with Portsmouth.

He later played for Swansea City and Bristol City before having a spell in the Vauxhall Conference with Yeovil. On hanging up his boots he became Football in the Community officer at Bristol Rovers.

CONSECUTIVE HOME GAMES

Brighton and Hove Albion played an extraordinary sequence of five home games in succession during the course of the 1978-79 season with the following results:

Date	Opponents	Result	Score
26.12.1978	Cardiff City	Won	5-0
30.12.1978	Newcastle United	Won	2-0
09.01.1979	Wolves (FA Cup)	Lost	2-3
20.01.1979	Stoke City	Drew	1-1
03.02 1979	Leicester City	Won	3-1

CONSECUTIVE SCORING – LONGEST SEQUENCE

Bobby Zamora holds the club record for consecutive scoring, achieved when he was on target in ten consecutive games during the 2000-01 season. He netted in the 2-2 draw at Notts County on 23 October 2001 and ended the sequence with a goal in another 2-2 draw at home to Chesterfield on 21 December 2001.

COOK, TOMMY

The club's leading goal scorer, Tommy Cook, was one of the few players from Division Three to have won full England honours and also one who played cricket successfully at county level. He began as a half-back but made his reputation as a centre forward with Albion, after being tried in this position for a month during which he scored two hat-tricks.

Cook made his Brighton debut in a goalless draw at Queen's Park Rangers in September 1922, going on to score six goals in eighteen outings to help the club finish in fourth place in the Third Division (South). In 1923-24 Cook and Hopkins formed a prolific strike partnership with the former scoring 28 goals in 37 League games. Included in this total were four in the 5-0 win over Bournemouth and hat-tricks in the wins against Aberdare Athletic (Home 5-0) Reading (Home 4-0) Everton (Home 5-2) and Newport County (Home 4-0).

Although not as prolific the following season, he still managed to score hat-tricks in successive matches as Newport County (Home 4-1) and Merthyr Town (Home 3-1) were beaten. Injuries hampered his progress in 1925-26 but the following season he was back at his best with 21 goals in 36 League games.

In 1927-28 Cook was again the club's leading scorer with 25 goals in

37 games, including a hat-trick in a 3-1 home win over Millwall. At the end of the following campaign, Cook, who had scored 123 goals in 209 games, left to take a cricket coaching post in South Africa.

Tommy Cook wearing his England cap.

During the 1929-30 season he returned to join Northfleet FC and in October 1931, Bristol Rovers secured his services. In just under two seasons he scored 21 goals in 43 appearances before retiring from football in 1933.

Cook was also a county cricketer and scored 20,906 runs for Sussex between 1922 and 1937. During the war he served in the South African Air Force and he was seriously injured in an accident which kept him in hospital for six months. After the war he returned to Brighton and was manager of the club for a short period.

CRICKETERS

The most notable cricketers to play for Brighton and Hove Albion are Tommy Cook and Ken Suttle. Tommy Cook, the holder of the club's League goal-scoring record, played in 459 first-class games for Sussex, scoring 20,906 runs at an average of 30.36 and a highest score of 278 made against Hampshire at Hove in 1930. He hit 32 centuries for Sussex and in 1934 scored 2,132 runs at 54.67.

Ken Suttle, who played in three League games for the Seagulls, scored 29,375 runs at 30.86 and had a top score of 204 not out against Kent at Tunbridge Wells in 1962.

CROWD TROUBLE

However unwelcome, crowd disturbances at major football matches are far from a modern phenomenon. Behaviour at Brighton matches in recent years has usually been of a high standard but there were occasions in the club's early years when incidents of crowd trouble occurred.

On 25 March 1905, in the match against West Ham United at the Goldstone Ground, Bertie Lyon put Albion 2-1 up just after the hour mark. As Lyon celebrated, the Hammers' England international keeper, Matt Kingsley, aimed a kick at him. The crowd, already incensed by the visitors' vigorous tactics, spilled on to the pitch and surrounded the West Ham players. Ugly scenes began to develop and only when order was restored, Kingsley dismissed, and Lyon carried to the changing room to receive treatment, did the game continue.

On 30 October 1920, the referee having blown for offside, changed his mind and allowed Luton's late equaliser against Albion at the Goldstone Ground. At the final whistle, the home fans swarmed across the pitch in the hope of gaining access to the referee's room. A policeman was hit on the head by someone throwing a corner flag but the misguided Albion fans dispersed when Jack Owen appealed to them to behave themselves and go home.

Not all the crowd trouble was at the Goldstone Ground. On 22 March 1965, in Albion's game at Rochdale, a number of Brighton players were subjected to a dreadful pelting from the Spotland crowd. Goalkeeper Brian Powney was hit by a dart and Barrie Rees just managed to avoid a flying china cup.

During the FA Cup second round tie against Northampton Town in December 1968, there was fighting in the North Stand. Closed circuit television had been installed for crowd supervision and as a result there were a number of arrests and convictions in the coming months. Towards the end of that season, the club was ordered to post warning notices around the ground after missiles had been thrown onto the pitch in the game against Hartlepool United. The following season both matches against Luton Town were marred by crowd trouble. After fighting in the North Stand, Albion's so-called supporters damaged turnstiles and sprayed paint on the walls of the Kenilworth Road ground, and smoke bombs were thrown from the terraces.

During the 1971-72 season, television cameras were installed for the Boxing Day match against Bournemouth but in a near riot there were still 29 arrests. Yet this was nothing compared to the visit by Spurs to the

Goldstone Ground on 15 April 1978. There were 51 arrests and 85 casualties with a quarter of them ending up in hospital. After the Spurs supporters infiltrated the North Stand, fighting spilled onto the pitch and the referee had no alternative but to take the teams off. When they came back on, Albion went on to win 3-1. However, the day's events prompted the FA to order the erection of a perimeter fence around the Goldstone pitch.

The worst outbreak of violence at the Goldstone Ground occurred on 3 September 1983. At the final whistle, Chelsea fans, who had infiltrated all parts of the ground, invaded the pitch to launch a cowardly attack on hopelessly outnumbered police. By the time mounted police had cleared the pitch, seven policemen had been injured and the north goal broken. The Minister for Sport, Neil Macfarlane, called for reports and both clubs were charged by the FA but cleared of blame.

CURBISHLEY, ALAN

A midfield play-maker who played for England schoolboys and England youth, Alan Curbishley was a member of the West Ham side which reached the FA Youth Cup Final in 1975. He went on to appear in almost a hundred games for the Hammers but he failed to beat off the competition of Brooking and Devonshire and left Upton Park to join Birmingham City and he helped them win promotion to Division One in 1979-80. There followed spells for Aston Villa and Charlton Athletic before he joined Brighton and Hove Albion in August 1987.

He made his debut in a goalless draw at Chesterfield, going on to score six goals in 34 games as the Seagulls won promotion to the Second Division as runners-up to Sunderland. Curbishley became the club's regular penalty taker the following season, scoring from the spot in three

Alan Curbishley.
Photo: Lancashire Evening Post.

successive games. In 1989-90 he missed only one game, taking his total of appearances, in which he scored 15 goals, to 128 before rejoining Charlton Athletic.

In 1991-92 Curbishley was appointed joint-manager of the Addicks with Steve Gritt. Despite problems with grounds and injuries, Charlton narrowly missed the Second Division play-offs. They made an emotional return to The Valley in December 1992 and three years later, Curbishley was appointed manager when Steve Gritt left. Now in their second spell in the Premiership, Charlton have one of the League's longest-serving managers in Alan Curbishley.

CURRY, BILL

An outstanding product of Newcastle schools football, Bill Curry became the first Magpies' player to graduate from the club's new junior set up. As a teenager, he once netted eight goals for Newcastle United in an FA

Bill Curry.

Youth Cup victory. When doing his National Service he appeared for the Army Select XI and scored five goals against the Navy in 1958. Despite being the first Newcastle player to be chosen for the England Under 23 side, he spent much of his time at St James Park as Len White's understudy and in July 1959 he joined Brighton and Hove Albion.

He made his Seagulls' debut in a 2-1 home defeat at the hands of Aston Villa on the opening day of the 1959-60 season, going on to be the club's leading scorer with 23 goals in 40 games.No one else reached double figures. His total included hat-tricks in the wins over Portsmouth (Home 3-1) and Bristol City (Home 5-1) and another treble in the fourth round FA Cup replay against Rotherham United which Albion won 6-0. He scored in each of the first three games of the 1960-61 season but after netting 29 goals in 54 games, left to join Derby County.

Curry continued to find the net on a regular basis for the Rams, scoring

67 goals in 148 League games. He later played for Mansfield Town and Chesterfield before managing non-League clubs Boston United and Sutton Town.

CURTIS, GEORGE

George Curtis began his League career with Arsenal, playing for the Gunners before and after the Second World War, during which he served in India as a corporal in the Royal Air Force. Midway through the 1946-47 season he was transferred to Southampton in part-exchange for Don Roper, and went on to become an important member of the early post-war Southampton sides.

On leaving The Dell he played for French club, Valenciennes, before returning to England as coach to the Cambridge University side. By this time he had become a qualified coach and held posts with both the England youth team and Sunderland before joining Brighton and Hove Albion as manager in the summer of 1961.

Curtis had an unhappy time at the Goldstone Ground as the Seagulls sank from the Second to the Fourth Division in two seasons. His teams were based on defence, which did not endear him to the Brighton faithful, and in February 1963 he left the club.

After a spell at Stevenage, he coached Hull City before moving to the United States to manage San Diego Toros, who reached the national finals of the first NASL. He then spent five years in Norway, three as national coach. Later he spent two years in Qatar, worked as a FIFA instructor in Japan, South Korea and other Far East countries.

D

DAVIE, JOCK

Signed from non-League Margate, centre-forward Jock Davie played his first game for the Albion in a 1-0 defeat at Gillingham on the opening day of the 1936-37 season. He scored both goals on his home debut four days later as Brighton beat Newport County 2-0. In only his fifteenth game for the club, he netted a hat-trick in a 4-0 win at Exeter City, but at the turn of the year the club's directors urged the recall of the more experienced Alec Law to lead the attack at Davie's expense. He returned towards the end of the season to finish with 13 goals in 24 games.

Forming a prolific partnership with Bert Stephens, Davie scored 17 goals in 38 outings in 1937-38. This total included four goals in a second round FA Cup replay win over South Liverpool, the non-League side being beaten 6-0 and a hat-trick in the first round as Tunbridge Wells were defeated 5-1. Although hampered by injuries the following season, he had scored 58 goals in 105 games on the outbreak of the Second World War.

During the hostilities, Davie was loaned to Queen's Park Rangers and repaid Albion's generosity by netting a hat-trick against his club mates in a 5-2 win for Rangers. However, he did score 55 goals in 76 wartime games for Brighton including five in an 8-2 win over Chelsea in 1941-42. When League football resumed in 1946-47, Davie could not force his way into the Albion side and left for Barnsley where he played a handful of games before retiring.

DEATH

Wing-half Barrie Rees, who had been chosen as reserve for the Welsh Under 23 side on a number of occasions and was widely tipped as a future full international, was travelling to his parents' home in Rhyl when his car was in collision with a lorry on the A5. Rees, who had scored in

36

the 4-4 draw with Chester and made 12 League appearances with Brighton, died in the Manor Hospital at Nuneaton from his injuries the next day.

DEFEATS – FEWEST

Brighton and Hove Albion suffered just six defeats in 2001-02 on their way to winning the Second Division Championship.

DEFEATS – MOST

A total of 26 defeats suffered during the season of 1995-96 is the worst in the Brighton's history. Not surprisingly they were relegated to the Third Division.

DEFEATS – WORST

Brighton and Hove Albion's record defeat came on 23 August 1958 when they travelled to Middlesbrough and were beaten 9-0. Their worst home defeat was 8-2 by Bristol Rovers on 1 December 1973. Plymouth Argyle had won 6-0 at the Goldstone Ground on 18 November 1950.

DEFENSIVE RECORDS

Brighton and Hove Albion's best defensive record was established in seasons 1922-23 and 1984-85 when in each campaign they conceded 34 goals from their 42 match programme.
The club's worst defensive record was in 1958-59 when they let in 90 goals but they still managed to finish in mid-table in Division Two.

DIGWEED, PERRY

Goalkeeper Perry Digweed was an apprentice when he started his Football League career with Fulham but had to wait two-and-a-half years for a second game.

In January 1981 he was transferred to Brighton and Hove Albion for £150,000, replacing the out-of-form Graham Moseley. He played in the last 15 games of the season, producing a number of saves that helped the club retain its top flight status. Digweed was to spend thirteen seasons at the Goldstone Ground, where his career was littered with a series of niggling injuries and loan spells with West Bromwich Albion, Charlton Athletic, Newcastle United and Chelsea.

After sharing the goalkeeping duties with Graham Moseley, he failed to make any appearances in 1984-85 and 1987-88, this latter season seeing the club promoted to Division Two.

He was the club's first-choice keeper in 1990-91, his displays helping Albion reach the play-offs and saw him voted 'Player of the Season'. He went on to appear in 201 League and Cup games for Brighton before being transferred to Wimbledon. After failing to make an appearance for the Dons, he joined Watford where further injuries finally curtailed his career.

DISMISSALS

A number of players have been sent off when playing for Brighton. One of the most infamous dismissals occurred on 1 December 1909 in the Southern League match against Norwich City. 'Bullet' Jones, Albion's prolific goal scorer, received his marching orders after former Brighton goalkeeper, Bob Beale, and his replacement between the posts, Charlie Craig, were both carried from the field injured after clashes with Jones. The Brighton centre-forward, who also had words with the referee, was suspended for two months.

DORAN, JACK

Jack Doran began his career with Norwich City but when Charlie Webb discovered that former England international George Holley's career was at an end, he brought the Canaries' centre-forward to the Goldstone Ground. Doran scored on his Southern League debut in a 4-2 home win over Swansea Town and ended the campaign with 10 goals in ten games, including a hat-trick in a 3-0 defeat of Southend United.

He made his Football League debut against the same opposition and although he failed to get on the scoresheet, he ended the season as top scorer with 21 goals, exactly half the club's total.

In 1921-22, the Irish international achieved a unique scoring feat with Albion. He collected all their first 12 Division Three (South) goals including hat-tricks in fixtures against Exeter City, (Home 3-1) and (Away 3-0).

By the end of November he had netted 17 goals in 13 games, including five in the 7-0 thrashing of Northampton Town. He was injured over the Christmas period and had to miss ten games, ending the season with a total of 23 goals in 31 games.

Doran, who had scored 55 goals in 85 games for Albion, was then transferred to First Division Manchester City for £1,050 but there he was unable to make much of an impact.

Jack Doran.
Photo: Chris Horlock

DRAWS

Brighton and Hove Albion played their greatest number of drawn League matches in a single season in 1948-49 when eighteen of their matches ended all square. Their fewest drawn League matches were in 1936-37 when only five of their matches were drawn. The club's highest scoring draw was 5-5, achieved in the FA Cup qualifying round against Gray's Athletic on 1 November 1902.

The club has also drawn five League games – 4-4 v Swindon Town (Division Three South on 29 September 1934) v Reading (Division Three South on 20 April 1935) v Chester (Division Four on 6 February 1965) v Leyton Orient (Division Three on 8 March 1997) and v Colchester United (Division Three on 26 December 1997).

39

DUBLIN, KEITH

England youth international defender Keith Dublin began his career with Chelsea before signing for Brighton in the summer of 1987. He made his debut in the opening game of the 1987-88 season as Albion beat York City 1-0 and, along with Steve Gatting, was ever-present as the club won promotion to the Second Division. Dublin missed very few games over the next two seasons, his displays at the heart of the Albion defence helping them maintain their place in Division Two. He was voted 'Player of the Season' in 1989-90 but left in the close season, joining Watford for £275,000.

Dublin, who had scored six goals in 146 games for Albion, was a virtual ever-present for the Hornets in four seasons at Vicarage Road before moving to Southend United. Capable in the air, speedy and safe on the ground, he was used as more of a utility player at Roots Hall and was club captain in most of his 198 games for the Shrimpers. He had loan spells with Colchester United and Canvey Island before being released in the summer of 1999.

E

EARLY GROUNDS

Brighton and Hove Albion trace their origins to a club called Brighton United which first played at the Sussex County Cricket Ground in 1898. When it was asked to leave two years later, Brighton and Hove Rangers were formed in its place and played on a field at Home Farm, Withdean. In September 1901, the Rangers, now reconstituted as Brighton and Hove Albion, returned to the cricket ground. Meanwhile, another local side, Hove FC, had found an ideal spot for a ground at Goldstone Bottom.

EVER-PRESENTS

Fifty-six Brighton players have been ever-presents throughout a Football League season. The greatest number of ever-present seasons by a Brighton player are four by both Eric Gill and Jack Bertolini. Next in line are Billy Hayes, Glen Wilson and Peter O'Sullivan with three.

In 1908 Albion supporters had undercover parking for their bicycles behind the South Stand at the Goldstone ground. Motorcyclists and car owners were not so well catered for as this postcard of that period shows.

F

FA CUP

During their early days in the Southern League, Albion reached the competition proper for the first time in 1905-06. They were exempted to the fourth qualifying round in which they travelled north to play Second Division, Glossop. This was the first time Albion had played Football League opposition in the FA Cup and a goal from Billy Yates was enough to separate the teams. In the first round, Swindon Town were beaten 3-0 to set up a home tie against First Division high-fliers Middlesbrough. Jimmy Kennedy scored an equalising goal just minutes from time, and in the replay four days later, the scores were again 1-1 after extra time. A second replay was staged at Bramall Lane but Middlesbrough won 3-1.

In 1907-08, Albion faced Preston North End in the first round of the FA Cup. Following a 1-1 draw at the Goldstone, the replay had to be abandoned during extra time with Albion leading 2-1. The match was deemed to be a 1-1 draw, the score after ninety minutes, but in the third meeting at Stamford Bridge, a goal from Dick Wombwell gave Albion a 1-0 win. In round two, Albion were drawn away to Liverpool, coming back from Anfield with a magnificent 1-1 draw. Sadly, in the replay, Liverpool proved too strong, winning 3-0.

In 1913-14, Albion were drawn away to Oldham Athletic who went on to finish fourth in Division One and were runners-up in the top flight in 1914-15. The Latics side contained several internationals but Albion managed to force a 1-1 draw at Boundary Park with Bill Miller scoring the equaliser in the seventy eighth minute. In the replay four days later, neither side had scored after ninety minutes and Billy Booth netted the game's only goal in extra time, with just seven minutes remaining.

Clapton Orient were Albion's second round opponents and two goals from Charlie Webb helped them to a 3-1 victory. When drawn away to Sheffield Wednesday, Albion had the better of the first half but failed to score and Wednesday, with three late goals, went through.

In 1922-23, Brighton were drawn at home to the legendary amateur club, Corinthians, a mostly public school and university side making its first entry into the FA Cup. An exciting match ended all-square at 1-1 at the Goldstone Ground, as did the replay four days later. The third meeting at Stamford Bridge was won 1-0 by Albion with Tommy Cook netting the decider. The club's reward was a home tie against First Division West Ham United. At a fog-shrouded Goldstone, Cook again found the net in a 1-1 draw. Unfortunately, despite a brave rearguard action in the Upton Park replay, the Hammers won 1-0.

In the following season, Albion faced Barnsley in the first round on a heavy Oakwell pitch. They did most of the attacking but the Yorkshire club's amateur keeper, Harold Cope, was in magnificent form and the game was goalless. In the replay, Jimmy Hopkins broke the deadlock with five minutes to play.

First Division Everton were Albion's opponents in the second round and were expected to win the tie but Albion were inspired and with Tommy Cook netting a hat-trick, beat the Toffees 5-2. In the third round, Manchester City were Albion's opponents at the Goldstone Ground but after Jimmy Hopkins had what appeared to be a good goal disallowed for offside, the Blues ran riot, winning 5-1.

In 1929-30, Albion beat Southern League opposition in rounds one and two as Peterborough United (Home 4-0) and Barry Town (Home 4-1)

The team that faced Everton in the second round of the FA Cup in 1924.
Photo: Chris Horlock.

43

were brushed aside. Albion's opponents in the third round were Grimsby Town and after a 1-1 draw, Hugh Vallance netted the only goal in the Blundell Park replay. Vallance was on target again in round four as Albion won 1-0 at Portsmouth. The fifth round saw Brighton travel to St James Park to take on Newcastle United where Hughie Gallacher scored a hat-trick in a 3-0 win for the Magpies.

In 1932-33, Brighton played 11 FA Cup games including replays and scored 43 goals without getting past round five. They forgot to claim exemption and had to play from the first qualifying round. In one of these matches, Arthur Attwood scored six times in a 12-0 defeat of Shoreham.

The club's next best cup run was in 1959-60. A 1-0 win at Southern League leaders Bath City gave Albion a fourth round trip to Rotherham United. The Millers, who had beaten Arsenal in round three, were held to two 1-1 draws before a Bill Curry hat-trick helped Albion to a 6-0 win in the third meeting at Highbury. In round five, Albion visited Deepdale to take on First Division Preston North End and though they put up a brave fight, they lost 2-1.

In 1982-83, Albion entertained Second Division Newcastle United in the third round. After a 1-1 draw, Albion travelled to St James Park for the replay as the underdogs and won 1-0, thanks to a Peter Ward goal. Manchester City were Albion's opponents in the fourth round but they were well beaten 4-0 with Michael Robinson netting two of Albion's goals. A visit to Anfield in round five was Albion's reward. Gerry Ryan put Brighton ahead before Craig Johnston levelled the scores in the seventieth minute. Ex-Liverpool midfielder Jimmy Case's 25 yard shot took a wicked deflection off Ronnie Whelan to give Albion the lead. Phil Neal then missed a penalty for the Reds as Brighton clung on for a famous victory.

Albion, in the quarter-finals for the first time, were drawn at home to fellow strugglers Norwich City. In a game that was certainly not a classic, a Jimmy Case goal took them through to the semi-finals. Sheffield Wednesday were Brighton's opponents at Highbury. Jimmy Case was again on target after a quarter of an hour with a shot from 35 yards that went in off the underside of the bar. The Owls equalised just prior to the hour mark but Gordon Smith netted twelve minutes from time to take Brighton through to their first FA Cup final.

Manchester United were Albion's opponents and firm favourites to lift the coveted trophy. Yet on thirteen minutes, Gordon Smith headed the Seagulls in front. There was no further scoring until the fifty seventh minute when Stapleton levelled for United. Shortly afterwards, Ray Wilkins scored a memorable goal to put United 2-1 up but with four minutes to go, Gary Stevens shot Albion level. Into extra time and Gordon Smith looked odds on to score what would most surely have been the winner but he fired at Gary Bailey's legs. In the replay five days later, United controlled the game from start to finish and ran out winners 4-0.

In 1985-86, Albion reached the quarter-finals after beating Newcastle United (Away 2-0) Hull City (Away 3-2) and Peterborough United (Home 1-0 after a 2-2 draw). Their opponents in the last eight were Southampton who won the Goldstone encounter 2-0. It was the club's last decent run in the competition.

FA CUP FINAL

Although now in their fourth season in the First Division, few could believe that the Seagulls had made it all the way to Wembley to take on the mighty Manchester United. However, Brighton had to play the final without their inspirational captain Steve Foster. He was suspended because of a booking in a League match and despite taking his case to the High Court, was forced to sit on the sidelines as Albion enjoyed the biggest day in their history.

And enjoy it they did. As the underdogs and already relegated from the top flight, they had nothing to lose. For much of the first half, the Seagulls played composed and relaxed football. Brighton's lead at the interval, courtesy of Gordon Smith's fourteenth minute header was well deserved. In the second-half, Manchester United got a grip on the game and goals from Frank Stapleton and Ray Wilkins gave them the lead. But then Jimmy Case intervened. His corner three minutes from time was pulled back to Tony Grealish who stabbed the ball into the path of Gary Stevens and the game was all-square.

In extra time, Brighton should have won the Cup just before the end when Michael Robinson set up Smith with a great chance. But just as the nation thought that Seagulls had pulled off a miracle, Smith hesitated and Gary Bailey saved the day. In the replay, and despite the return of Steve

45

Foster, Brighton were beaten 4-0 by a United side which was in no mood to flirt with humiliation again.

FAMOUS FANS

The club's most famous fan has to be football presenter Des Lynam. During the 1992-93 season, when the club were in a perilous financial situation, Des Lynam set up an SOS (Save Our Seagulls) fund in an attempt to pay off its creditors. In conjunction with the local radio station Southern FM, Des helped to raise around £28,500 in a marathon broadcast on Sunday 25 April 1993 with more planned events to follow.

FARRELL, BOBBY

Winger Bobby Farrell joined Brighton from Portsmouth in the summer of 1928, making his debut in a 3-1 defeat at Norwich City. Over the next few seasons, his pinpoint crosses created numerous scoring opportunities for Dan Kirkwood, Hugh Vallance and Arthur Attwood as Albion pressed for promotion from the Third Division (South).

Although not a prolific scorer, Farrell did find the net on 16 occasions in 1932-33 including a hat-trick in a 9-0 win at Hastings and St Leonard's in an FA Cup qualifying round match. He was a regular member of the Brighton side up until the outbreak of the Second World War and had scored 84 goals in 430 games for Albion by the start of the hostilities. He continued to play for the club during the early war years, netting hat-tricks against Chelsea (Home 5-1) and Southampton (Home 9-4).

FESTIVAL OF BRITAIN

In May 1951, Albion won all three of its games in the Festival of Britain. The matches, which were all played at the Goldstone Ground, saw Brighton beat Nancy of France 2-1, Hamborn 07 of Germany 3-2 and Scotland's Ayr United 5-1.

FIRST DIVISION

Brighton have had just one spell of four seasons in the top flight of the Football League. After winning promotion as runners-up to Crystal

Action from Brighton's first game in the top flight – against Arsenal.
Photo: Lancashire Evening Post.

Palace in 1978-79, they knew they would have to strengthen their defence to compete at the highest level and so Steve Foster of Portsmouth for £150,000 and John Gregory of Aston Villa for a record £250,000 joined the club.

Albion's first game in Division One saw them beaten 4-0 at home by Arsenal but after two away defeats, they gained their first success in the top flight, beating Bolton Wanderers 3-1. However, by mid-November they were bottom of the table and had been written off, when they had an unbeaten run of seven matches and finished in sixteenth place.

In 1980-81, Albion fared little better and in spite of three successive victories over the Christmas period, they continued to hover just above the three relegation places. Then, after beating Coventry City 4-1 at the beginning of March, they took two points from five games to put them in the bottom three with four games to play.

Relegation looked highly probable but after a 2-0 win at already

47

demoted Crystal Palace, there was hope. Albion then beat Leicester City 2-1 and Sunderland by the same score to leave them needing a win against Leeds United on the last day of the season. Goals from Foster and Ritchie gave Albion a 2-1 triumph and four successive victories at the end of the season.

Albion had their best season in the First Division in 1981-82 – when three points for a win was introduced. Their early form was good and included a 4-1 home victory over Manchester City with Andy Ritchie scoring twice. As the season unfolded, the club reached eighth place and were hopeful of a UEFA Cup place but after winning only two of their last fourteen games, had to be satisfied with thirteenth place.

In 1982-83, Brighton made it all the way to the FA Cup Final but yet still lost their First Division status. Their home form was quite good but they won just one away game – a 2-1 victory at Swansea, who were also relegated. Even so, victory in the final game of the season against Manchester City could still have provided a slender lifeline, but Albion lost 1-0 and finished the season in bottom place.

FIRST LEAGUE MATCH

Brighton's first Football League match saw them travel to the Kursaal Ground to take on the home side, Southend United on 28 August 1920. The Seagulls' captain, Jack Rutherford, had been injured in a pre-season trial game and so Jack Woodhouse skippered the side in his absence. The Shrimps won 2-0 against a Brighton side of:

Billy Hayes, Jack Woodhouse, Wally Little, Fretwell Hall, George Coomber, Harry Bentley, Bert Longstaff, George Ritchie, Jack Doran, Ted Rogerson and Zacky March.

FIRST MATCH

Brighton and Hove Albion's first match was a friendly against Shoreham at Dyke Road Field on 7 September 1901. The Brighton side was:

Squire Whitehurst, Donald Coles, Jack Caldwell, Paddy Farrell, Jim Sutherland, F.Mitchell, C.J.Mendham, Clem Barker, Frank McAvoy (Captain), W Smith and Edgar Ffennel.

48

For the record, Albion won 2-0 with the goals scored by Barker and McAvoy.

FLOODLIGHTS

Brighton and Hove Albion were one of the last Football League clubs to install floodlights – in 1961 with the Drenchliting system at a cost of £13,523. The new lights were first switched on for the friendly match against nine times champions of Denmark, Boldklubben of Copenhagen, on 10 April 1961. Despite atrocious weather, a crowd of 7,541 braved the elements and turned out to see Albion win an entertaining encounter 3-1.

FOOTBALL LEAGUE CUP

The Football League Cup was born in 1960 and was the brainchild of Alan Hardaker who was the secretary of the Football League for more than twenty years. It was a competition designed exclusively for the ninety two League clubs with a two-legged final to be played home and away at the grounds of the finalists.

At the outset, the competition met with much criticism. It was condemned for adding another burden to the already congested fixture list and six of the big clubs refused to enter. Brighton won their first match in the contest, beating Notts County 3-1 with Adrian Thorne netting twice, before losing 2-0 at home to Fourth Division Wrexham.

Albion reached the fourth round of the League Cup for the first time in 1966-67, beating Leyton Orient (Home 1-0) Norwich City (Away 1-0) and Coventry City (Away 3-1 after a 1-1 draw) before they met Northampton Town and were held to a 1-1 draw at the Goldstone Ground. In the replay at the County Ground, Albion suffered what was their heaviest defeat in the competition, the Cobblers winning 8-0.

Brighton reached the fourth round again in 1976-77. After beating Southend United over two legs (Home 2-1 Away 1-1) they travelled to Portman Road to take on First Division Ipswich Town. A superb rearguard action prevented an Ipswich side packed with internationals from scoring before goals from Binney and Cross gave the Seagulls a 2-1 victory in the replay. In the third round, Albion again faced First Division opposition in West Bromwich Albion but two goals from leading scorer, Peter Ward, took them through to the fourth round and a meeting with mighty Derby County. Peter Ward scored after just 37 seconds but the Rams equalised to force a replay. At the Baseball Ground, Ian Mellor scored for Albion but the home side won 2-1.

In 1978-79, Albion progressed to the last eight of the League Cup for the first time. A Peter O'Sullivan goal was enough to beat Millwall in round two before Peter Ward netted twice in a 3-1 win at Burnley. In round four, Albion completely dominated Peterborough United but only won 1-0, thanks to a Mark Lawrenson goal. In the fifth round for the first time, Albion travelled to Nottingham Forest, League Champions and current holders of the League Cup. Forest, who won that season's European Cup, beat Brighton 3-1. This remains Brighton's best performance in the competition.

FOREIGN OPPOSITION

In their first match against foreign opposition, Brighton and Hove Albion defeated Athletique Parisien 9-1 on Boxing Day 1904 with Tom Robertson netting a hat-trick.

FOREMAN, DENNIS

South African-born winger Dennis Foreman scored on his debut in a 4-2 home win over Aldershot in October 1952. In the next couple of seasons he found himself in and out of the Albion side but when called upon to play, he netted a number of vital goals. It was 1953-54 before he won a regular place in the Brighton side, helping them to finish as runners-up in the Third Division (South).

Foreman netted his first hat-trick for the club in November 1955 as Albion beat Newport County 8-1 in a first round FA Cup tie. Although having his best season in terms of goals scored – 16 in 1956-57 – he was considered by many to be below his best. The following season he helped the club win the Third Division (South) Championship.

Unfortunately, after scoring the club's first Second Division goal, Foreman received a nasty leg injury which forced him to miss the rest of the campaign. He played in a handful of games in 1959-60 but it was clear that he was a shadow of his former self. It was a similar story the following season and in the summer of 1961, after scoring 69 goals in 219 games, he was released.

FORMATION

In November 1897, a professional club named Brighton United was formed at the Imperial Hotel, Queens Road, but in March 1900 after less than two seasons in the Southern League, playing at the County Ground, they folded. Then an amateur team by the name of Brighton and Hove Rangers was formed by a number of United supporters. After one season playing at Withdean, they decided to turn semi-professional and play at the County Ground. Rangers were also accepted into the Southern League but in the summer of 1901, they too folded.

The former manager of Brighton United, John Jackson organised a meeting at the Seven Stars public house on 24 June 1901 at which a third club, Brighton and Hove United was formed. They took over the Rangers' place in the Southern League and pitch at the County Ground.

The name was changed to Brighton and Hove Albion before a match was played, because of objections by Hove FC.

FOSTER, STEVE

A product of the Portsmouth youth side, Steve Foster made his League debut for the Fratton Park club during the 1975-76 season when Pompey finished bottom of Division Two. He had arrived as a centre-forward but manager Ian St John suggested a switch of position and he soon established himself at the heart of the club's defence.

In the summer of 1979 he was transferred to Brighton for £150,000 and made his debut in a 2-0 League Cup win over Cambridge United. His form for the Seagulls led to him being voted the club's 'Player of the Season' and winning full international honours, being capped three times by England.

An ever-present in 1980-81, he was outstanding as Albion just avoided relegation by winning their last four games of the season – Foster's only goal coming on the final day in a 2-0 defeat of Leeds United. He continued to turn in consistent performances and led Albion to the FA Cup Final in 1983. Unfortunately he was suspended and he missed the first match but returned for the replay which the Seagulls lost 4-0 to Manchester United.

In March 1984 he was transferred to Aston Villa but by the end of the year he had left to join Luton Town, winning a League Cup winners' medal in 1988. He then joined Oxford United before returning to Brighton for a second spell in the summer of 1992. He took his tally of goals to 12 in 245 games but was released following knee ligament damage that required surgery.

FOURTH DIVISION

Brighton have had only one spell of two seasons in the Fourth Division following their relegation to the League's basement at the end of the 1962-63 campaign. After taking one point in their opening four League games of 1963-64, they were third from bottom of the Fourth Division but then only two of the next 14 games ended in defeat. Despite a number of impressive away performances, Albion could not maintain the pressure on the leading pack and ended the season in eighth place.

In the close season they signed Spurs and England centre-forward Bobby Smith and he scored twice on the opening day of the 1964-65 season as Barrow was beaten 3-1. The Seagulls' home form was outstanding. They were unbeaten at the Goldstone Ground – the only time they have achieved that feat – and kept in contention for promotion throughout the season.

The final game saw Darlington visit the Goldstone. A point would see Brighton promoted, two points would clinch the title. A crowd of 31,423 saw Albion run out 3-1 winners.

FULL MEMBERS CUP

Brighton first entered the Full Members Cup, so called because it was originally open only to First and Second Division clubs, in 1985-86 but went out in the group stage to West Bromwich Albion (Home 1-2) despite winning 3-1 at Crystal Palace. In 1986-87, Albion went out at the first hurdle, losing 3-0 at home to Birmingham City.

G

GALL, NORMAN

Centre-half Norman Gall joined Brighton from non-League Gateshead midway through the 1962-63 season and made his League debut in a 2-0 defeat at Watford. He only made four appearances that season and was never on the winning side as Albion were relegated to the Fourth Division. After that he was the club's first-choice No.5 for the next ten seasons, only missing games through injury. In 1964-65, he helped Albion win the Fourth Division Championship, his only goal of the campaign being the winner in the 2-1 defeat of Tranmere Rovers.

When John Napier arrived at the Goldstone Ground, Gall filled in other defensive positions and during the course of the 1967-68 season, wore five different numbered shirts. Over the next few seasons he proved a valuable utility player and in November 1968, when Kit Napier netted a hat-trick against Bristol Rovers, it was Gall who wore the No.9 shirt.

When Brighton won promotion to the Second Division as runners-up to Aston Villa in 1971-72, Gall was ever-present at the heart of the Albion defence. He continued to be an integral member of the side for one more season, taking his total number of appearances, in which he scored four goals, to 488 before deciding to retire.

GATTING, STEVE

Younger brother of Middlesex and England cricketer, Mike Gatting, Steve began his career with Arsenal and was a valuable member of the squad which reached three consecutive FA Cup Finals. However, due to

53

the signing of Brian Talbot, his first team appearances became restricted and in September 1981 he was transferred to Brighton and Hove Albion for £180,000. He made his Seagulls' debut in a 1-1 draw at Everton, replacing the injured Gary Stevens, and remained at the heart of the Brighton defence for the next ten years.

Injuries hampered his progress in 1984-85 and he only returned to first team action midway through the following season. An ever-present in 1987-88 he was an influential member of the Brighton side that won an immediate return to Division Two as runners-up to Sunderland.

Injuries again prevented him from playing in as many games as he would have liked over the next couple of seasons but when he left the Goldstone Ground in the summer of 1991, he had scored 20 goals in 364 League and Cup games. He joined Charlton Athletic and played in 64 League games for that club before leaving the first-class game.

GILL, ERIC

Goalkeeper Eric Gill made his Albion debut in a 3-1 home win over Leyton Orient, but he had to wait until towards the end of the 1952-53 season before establishing himself as the first-choice keeper. He was ever-present in the Brighton goal for four seasons during which he set the club record of 222 consecutive League appearances.

In 1953-54, he had an outstanding season as Albion finished runners-up to Ipswich Town in the Third Division (South) and was without doubt the club's most consistent player throughout the decade. He won a Third Division (South) Championship medal in 1957-58 but injuries were now hampering his progress and he found himself having to share the goalkeeper's jersey with Dave Hollins.

Gill, who played in 296 games for Brighton, was forced to leave the first-class scene at the end of the 1959-60 season.

GOALKEEPERS

Brighton and Hove Albion has been extremely well served by their goalkeepers and most of then have been popular with their supporters.

Bob Whiting was Albion's keeper when they won the Southern League Championship and FA Charity Shield in 1909-10. He was first-choice keeper from 1908 until the outbreak of the First World War, appearing in a total of 320 games for the club.

First keeper in the Football League was Billy Hayes, who made his debut in Albion's first game in the competition. Ever-present in three seasons, he played in 160 consecutive League games for Brighton and a total of 225 in all competitions.

Stan Webb replaced Walter Cook as Albion's first-choice goalkeeper midway through the 1925-26 season but it was 1928-29 before he won a permanent place. He went on to appear in 234 games for Albion before losing his place to Charlie Thomson who had signed from Falkirk. He was the club's custodian until the outbreak of the Second World War, appearing in 191 games for Albion.

After the war goalkeeping duties were shared by Harry Baldwin and Jack Ball, who went on to appear in 183 and 118 games respectively. Eric Gill joined the club from Charlton Athletic in the summer of 1952 and helped the Seagulls win the Third Division (South) Championship in 1957-58 and was ever-present in four seasons. Brian Powney was only 17 years old when he made his Brighton debut in the final match of the 1961-62 season, a 2-0 defeat at Derby County. He was first-choice keeper for ten years, appearing in 386 games.

Former Nottingham Forest goalkeeper, Peter Grummitt, joined Albion on loan from Sheffield Wednesday before making the move a permanent one. He helped the club win promotion to the Second Division in 1976-77, keeping 16 clean sheets in 31 appearances before injury in the match against Tranmere Rovers ended his career.

Graham Moseley kept a clean sheet on his debut as Malcolm Poskett netted a hat-trick in a 4-0 win over Bristol Rovers. During the club's promotion-winning season of 1978-79, he shared the goalkeeping duties with Eric Steele before becoming first-choice midway through Brighton's first top flight season. Moseley, who kept goal for Albion in the 1983 FA Cup Final matches against Manchester United, made 224 appearances before losing out to Perry Digweed. An athletic goalkeeper, Digweed made 201 first team appearances before joining Wimbledon and later Watford.

GOALS – CAREER BEST

The highest goal scorer in the club's history is Tommy Cook who, between 1921 and 1929, netted 123 goals for the club – 114 in the League and nine in the FA Cup.

Bert Stephens did score 174 goals in all competitions but 78 of these came in war-time matches.

GOALS – INDIVIDUAL

Two players have scored five goals for Brighton in a Football League game. The first to do so was Jack Doran in a 7-0 win over Northampton Town on 5 November 1921. The feat was repeated by Adrian Thorne on 30 April 1958 when the Seagulls beat Watford 6-0.

Two players have scored six goals in a match for Brighton. Arthur Attwood did so in the 12-0 FA Cup win over non-League Shoreham on 1 October 1932 and Don Welsh, when guesting during the Second World War, did so on 22 March 1941 in the 7-4 win over Luton own.

GOALS – SEASON

The club's highest goal scorer in League matches in any one season is Peter Ward who scored 32 League goals in 1976-77 when the club finished runners-up to Mansfield Town in the Third Division. He also scored three goals in the League Cup and one in the FA Cup.

GOAL SCORING EXPLOITS

Brighton's Irish international centre-forward Jack Doran is the only player in Football League history to score more than half their side's goals in a complete season on two occasions – and he did it in successive seasons. In 1920-21 he netted 22 of the club's 42 goals and in 1921-22, he scored 23 of Brighton's 45 goals.

GOLDSTONE GROUND

Hove FC opened the Goldstone Ground on 7 September 1901, the same day that Brighton and Hove Albion, playing for the first time under the new title, did so in a field on Dyke Road because the cricket ground was unavailable.

In February 1902, Albion should have played a home game on the cricket ground but could not because the pitch was already booked so Hove invited them to use the Goldstone Ground. After playing a number of games on it, a formal groundshare arrangement was agreed. Eventually, Hove FC sold the lease to Albion and moved back to Hove Park. At this time, there was a small pavilion on the west side of the ground and behind the south goal was a low wooden stand. Also, behind the Old Shoreham Road goal was a pond into which players would deliberately kick the ball in order to soften the leather.

By the end of the First World War the Goldstone Ground was almost derelict, so when the club was admitted to the Football League in 1920, extensive redevelopment was required. The pond was drained to make way for the North Bank, and in 1926 the club bought the ground for £8,000. The one proviso was that no structure above the height of 50ft could be built on the east side. Restrictions of this nature, and even tighter ones on commercial and industrial buildings to the south and west, led to frequent reports of Albion leaving the Goldstone.

In 1958 the West Stand was built at a cost of £30,000 and later that year Albion's largest crowd of 36,747 was recorded for the visit of Fulham. Only two-thirds of the stand project was carried out and, during the club's time in Division One, the gap that was left was filled with a temporary 974 seat structure, known rather sarcastically as the Lego Stand. In 1979 the North Stand roof was deemed unsafe and when it was taken down, there was no standing cover at all apart from the West Stand paddock.

Six years later the North Stand was re-roofed as part of a £1.2 million ground and safety improvement programme but after the Hillsborough disaster, the Goldstone Ground was effectively written off.

With mounting debts, and mounting frustration of not being able to find an alternative site, the club was caught in a trap. If it was to have a new stadium, it would have to sell the Goldstone for as much as possible in order to clear its debts and start building. After Hove Council turned down a planning application for a food store and garden centre on the ground, the club faced the first of several winding-up orders for non-payment of tax.

News leaked out that the ground had been sold to Chartwell Developments and that Albion was planning to ground-share with Portsmouth while a new site was found and developed. However, the

Football League, which had to sanction the proposal, refused to do so and at the eleventh hour the club agreed to lease back the Goldstone from Chartwell Developments for the 1996-97 season only.

On 26 April 1997, in their last match at the Goldstone, Albion beat Doncaster Rovers 1-0 and moved off the bottom of the League for the first time in 29 weeks, so tempering the fans' fury at their eviction after 95 years.

The following season early home games were played at Gillingham's Priestfield Stadium and in October 1998 the club returned to Brighton to play home matches at Withdean Sports Stadium in Tongdean Lane, with every one being all-ticket.

GOODCHILD, JOHNNY

Johnny Goodchild began his career with Sunderland, scoring 21 goals in 44 games including a hat-trick in a 4-1 defeat of Sheffield United before following Brighton's new manager George Curtis to the Goldstone Ground.

He scored twice on his debut in a 3-3 draw at Scunthorpe United on the opening day of the 1961-62 season, going on to end his first campaign as joint top scorer in the League with Bobby Laverick on 10 goals. Injuries and a loss of form hampered his progress in 1962-63 but he was back to his best the following season, heading the club's scoring charts with 14 goals. Moved out to the wing, Goodchild's crosses helped Wally Gould and new signing Bobby Smith score 40 goals between them in 1964-65 when Albion won the Fourth Division Championship. Not to be outdone, Goodchild scored 10 goals from the wing and was never on the losing side when he found the net. However, he was unable to hold down a regular place in the Third Division and, having scored 44 goals in 176 games, left to play for York City, later ending his career with Darlington.

GOODWIN, FRED

One of the Busby Babes, he was always overshadowed by Duncan Edwards and Eddie Colman at Old Trafford and consequently his appearances were rare. After the Munich Air Disaster, however, he was drafted into the side and soon became a key member. He played in the 1958 FA

Cup Final but after the arrival of Maurice Setters, he joined Leeds United. Tragically his career at Elland Road was ended by the triple fracture of one of his legs and he moved to Scunthorpe United where he later became manager.

In November 1968 he took over the reins at the Goldstone Ground and had two good seasons on the south coast, leading the Seagulls to fifth place in the Fourth Division in 1969-70. At the end of that season, he left to manage Birmingham City and took the Blues into the First Division in 1971-72 and to two losing FA Cup semi-finals in 1973 and 1975.

He later went on to become manager-coach of Minnesota Kicks and during the 1980s he recruited players for the American Indoor League.

GORDON, DENNIS

Winger Dennis Gordon was discovered playing non-League football for Oxford City by First Division West Bromwich Albion, who offered him the chance to turn professional. Unable to hold down a regular first team place at The Hawthorns, he moved to Brighton in the summer of 1952 and played his first game for the club in a 4-2 home defeat of Exeter City.

In 1953-54 he missed just one game as Brighton finished runners-up to Ipswich Town in the Third Division (South). That campaign saw him score ten goals as well as create numerous chances for the leading scorer, Bert Addinall.

Gordon's best season in terms of goals scored was 1954-55 when he netted 14 in 43 appearances. He continued to be an important member of the Brighton side for the next few seasons but injuries then began to restrict his appearances at first team level and at the end of the 1960-61 season, after scoring 68 goals in 293 League and Cup games, he decided to retire.

GOULD, WALLY

Winger Wally Gould played his early League football for Sheffield United, a club he had joined from local side Rawmarsh Welfare. Unable to make much of an impression at Bramall Lane, he left the Blades after just a handful of appearances to play for York City.

His goal-scoring wing play had a number of clubs after his services but it was Brighton he joined in January 1964. He made his Albion debut in a 1-1 draw at Stockport County that month and missed very few games over the next three seasons. In 1964-65 he was top scorer with 21 goals as Albion won the Fourth Division Championship, a point ahead of runners-up Millwall. He found it harder in the Third Division but still reached double figures in terms of goals scored and was joint-top scorer in 1966-67. Injuries then began to restrict his first team outings and he was forced into retirement after scoring 46 goals in 193 games – a remarkable total for an out-and-out winger.

GRITT, STEVE

In more than 400 League and Cup appearances for Charlton Athletic Steve Gritt played in every position except goalkeeper. A determined player who thrived on hard work, he was a member of the Charlton side that was relegated in 1979-80 but bounced back the following season and was promoted in third place. After helping the club win promotion to the top flight in 1985-86, Gritt was then in and out of the side. Many felt that his Charlton career had ended with his departure to Walsall but he soon returned to the club, his move coinciding with its return to The Valley. In July 1991 he and Alan Curbishley were appointed as joint managers of Charlton Athletic and in their first season the club just missed out on reaching the Second Division play-offs.

In December 1996, Steve Gritt took over the reins at the Goldstone Ground and at the same time the club was docked two points after two pitch invasions in the match against Lincoln in October. This left them 11 points adrift at the bottom of the League. Under Gritt's leadership, results started to improve and in the last match at the Goldstone Ground, Albion beat Doncaster 1-0 and moved off the bottom of the League. With little or no improvement in results the following season, Gritt was sacked in February 1998.

GRUMMITT, PETER

Goalkeeper Peter Grummitt began his League career with Nottingham Forest after joining the City Ground club from non-League Bourne Town in May 1960. After turning in a number of impressive displays in the club's Football Combination side, he made his League debut for Forest against Bolton Wanderers at the age of 18. His first touch of the ball was to pick it out of the net after Jim Iley had put through his own goal. He went on to represent the Football League and England at Under 23 level, but he never won a full cap – surely one of the best keepers never to have done so.

He was ever-present in 1966-67 when Forest reached the FA Cup semi-finals and finished runners-up in the First Division. Surprisingly, after 352 first team appearances, he was allowed to leave the City Ground and joined Sheffield Wednesday. After four seasons at Hillsborough, he joined the Seagulls on loan.

He did not have the best of debuts as Brighton lost 4-1 at Tranmere Rovers. The deal was soon made permanent but in 1974-75, Albion were nearly relegated to the Fourth Division, only Grummitt's heroics preventing them from entering the League's basement. An ever-present in 1975-76, keeping 17 clean sheets, Grummitt almost helped the Seagulls win promotion but they finished fourth. The following season, he was again in outstanding form and had played in 31 games, keeping 16 clean sheets when he was injured in the game against Tranmere Rovers and, after 158 appearances for Albion, never played again.

GUEST PLAYERS

The guest system was used by all clubs during both world wars. Although on occasions it was abused almost beyond belief – some sides that opposed Brighton had ten or eleven guests – it normally worked sensibly and effectively and to the benefit of players, clubs and supporters.

The club had a number of famous guests, including Chelsea and England internationals Sam Weaver and Vic Woodley and Spurs' Welsh wing-half Ron Burgess. Charlton Athletic's Don Welsh, later to become Brighton manager, scored 17 goals in nine games for Albion, including six in a 7-4 defeat of Luton Town on 22 March 1941.

H

HALL, JACK

Jack Hall joined Brighton from Stoke in the summer of 1906. A prolific goal scorer with the Potters, he made his debut for the south coast club at Leyton on the opening day of the 1906-07 season, scoring the game's only goal. He went on to top the club's scoring charts with 22 goals in 37 Southern League games, helping Albion to finish in third place. Included in that total was a hat-trick on his home debut as Luton Town were beaten 7-2. The following season, Hall was again the club's top scorer with 16 goals. At the end of that season, the club received an offer from Middlesbrough that it could not refuse and Jack Hall, who had scored 46 goals in 82 first team appearances, moved to Ayresome Park.

In three seasons in the north-east, Hall even outscored Steve Bloomer before leaving to end his career with Leicester Fosse. He later coached both Feyenoord and PSV Eindhoven before ending his involvement with the game.

HARBURN, PETER

Peter Harburn, an amateur forward with the Royal Navy, was given a chance in League football towards the end of the 1954-55 season, making his debut in a 1-1 draw at Gillingham. He played in nine games, scoring three goals, including a double in a 5-3 home win over Aldershot.

In 1955-56, when Albion finished runners-up to Leyton Orient in the Third Division (South), Harburn formed a prolific partnership with Albert Mundy. He scored 27 League and Cup goals including four in the 8-1 first round FA Cup victory over Newport County. He continued to find the net with great regularity and he topped the club's scoring charts with 20 goals as Albion won the Third Division (South) Championship.

At the end of that season Harburn, who had scored 65 goals in 133 games, left to join First Division Everton.

Unable to hold down a regular place at Goodison Park, he moved to Scunthorpe United but less than a year later, he was on the move again, this time to Workington where he ended his first-class career.

HAT-TRICKS

Irish international forward Jack Doran achieved a unique scoring feat of its kind with Brighton in the 1921-22 season – he collected all their first 12 Division Three (South) goals. He also scored hat-tricks on successive Wednesdays for Albion against Exeter City (Away 3-0 and Home 3-1). The treble at St James Park was the club's first in the Football League.

The honour of scoring the club's fastest hat-trick falls to Adrian Thorne. The local-born striker netted his treble in the space of just four minutes in the final match of the club's Third Division (South) Championship winning season of 1957-58 as the Seagulls beat Watford 6-0. In fact, Thorne scored five of the club's goals that day.

Two players have scored double hat-tricks for the club, but neither were in the Football League. Arthur Attwood first achieved the feat on 1 October 1932 as Brighton beat Shoreham 12-0 in an FA Cup qualifying round tie. Don Welsh, guesting for the club during the Second World War, netted six of Brighton's goals in a 7-4 win over Luton Town on 22 March 1941.

Two Brighton players hold the record for the most hat-tricks in their careers with the Seagulls – Tommy Cook and Jock Davie have both netted eight trebles, although four of the latter's were during wartime games.

HAYES, BILLY

Goalkeeper Billy Hayes played in a number of games for Preston North End before the First World War, joining Albion at the start of the 1919-20 Southern League season in which he was ever-present. He was the club's keeper when they played their inaugural Football League game at Southend United, going on to miss just one game. An ever-present in 1921-22 when he kept 12 clean sheets, he was outstanding as Albion eventually succeeded in avoiding having to apply for re-election.

The following season he was again ever-present, helping Albion finish fourth in the Third Division (South) with a series of outstanding displays which included 19 clean sheets. Hayes was improving with each season and in 1923-24 kept a record 22 clean sheets including seven in a row. He played in 225 games for Albion, including 175 consecutive League and Cup games – a record until broken by Eric Gill in September 1956 – before leaving to end his career with Southend United.

HENDERSON, STEWART

Full-back Stewart Henderson was on Chelsea's books for a year without making the grade prior to joining Brighton and Hove Albion in the summer of 1965. He had to bide his time in the club's reserve side for several months before making his League debut in a 3-1 defeat at Shrewsbury Town in May 1966. The following season he shared the right-back duties with Jimmy Magill, and in 1967-68 injuries ruled him out of contention until the latter stages of the campaign.

Henderson missed very few games in 1968-69 and scored the only goal of his Brighton career in the 6-0 rout of Oldham Athletic. The following season Albion pushed hard for promotion with Henderson, missing just one game, having an outstanding campaign. He continued to be the club's first-choice right-back until March 1972 when, after appearing in 226 games, he was allowed to join Reading.

He spent eight seasons at Elm Park, scoring six goals in 166 League games before hanging up his boots.

HOME MATCHES

Brighton's best home win is the 14-2 rout of Brighton Amateurs in a qualifying round FA Cup tie on 4 October 1902. The club has netted nine goals in a League game on two occasions – against Newport County on 18 April 1951 and Southend United on 27 November 1965. The worst home defeat was 8-2, a scoreline inflicted on the side by Bristol Rovers on 1 December 1973.

HOME SEASONS

Brighton and Hove Albion have gone through a complete League season with an undefeated home record on just one occasion – 1964-65 – when they won the Fourth Division Championship. Albion's highest number of home wins in a season is 20 in 1955-56 when they finished runners-up in the Third Division (South).

HONOURS

The major honours achieved by the club are:

FOOTBALL LEAGUE

Second Division Champions	2001-02
Third Division Champions	2000-01
Third Division Runners-up	1971-72 1976-77 1987-88
Third Division (South) Champions	1957-58
Third Division (South) Runners-up	1953-54 1955-56
Fourth Division Champions	1964-65

FA CUP

FA Cup Runners-up	1983

HOPKINS, JIMMY

Inside-forward Jimmy Hopkins played his early football for Belfast United before joining Arsenal soon after the First World War. He scored on his League debut for the Gunners in a 4-3 win over West Bromwich Albion but afterwards his career was affected by spells of injury and illness and in January 1923 he was transferred to Brighton and Hove Albion.

He made his Seagulls' debut in a 2-1 win at Watford, going on to score five goals in 17 games in the second-half of the 1922-23 season. Forming a prolific strike force with Tommy Cook, Hopkins netted 20 goals the following season including hat-tricks in the wins over Portsmouth (Away 3-1) and Norwich City (Home 3-0).

Although not as prolific a scorer over the ensuing seasons, his form was such that he was capped at full international level by Northern Ireland. He was plagued by injuries during the course of the 1926-27 season but returned to net another hat-trick in the 7-0 demolition of Bristol Rovers. After that, he continued to score on a more regular basis and had netted 75 goals in 233 League and Cup games when at the end of the 1928-29 season, he moved into the Southern League with Aldershot.

HORTON, BRIAN

Master of the well-timed tackle and interception, wing-half Brian Horton began his League career with Port Vale whom he joined from Hednesford Town in 1970. He had appeared in 258 games for the Valiants when in March 1976 he joined Brighton and Hove Albion for £30,000 and became synonymous with the Seagulls' rise from the Third to the First Division.

Wing-half Brian Horton at speed.
Photo: Lancashire Evening Post.

He made his debut in a 1-0 defeat at Preston North End and he was impressive in the eleven games he played at the end of the 1975-76 season, when the club just missed out on promotion to the Second Division. Appointed captain, he skippered the side to Division Two in 1976-77 and then after almost successive promotions, led them to the top flight in 1978-79. In fact, Horton was the club's leading scorer that season with 11 goals. An ever-present in Albion's first-ever season of First Division football, he went on to score 41 goals in 252 games before joining Luton Town.

He was an instant success at Kenilworth Road but later left to become player-manager of Hull City. In 1984-85 he led the Tigers to promotion to the Second Division but a string of poor results later cost him his job.

In 1988 he took charge of Oxford United, later managing Manchester City and Huddersfield Town before taking charge at Brighton. After a year at the helm he returned to Vale Park to manage the Valiants.

HOWARD, FRANKIE

Frankie Howard played his early football for non-League Guildford City before joining Brighton as an amateur in 1948. It was some time before he signed professional forms, Howard making his League debut in a 1-1 draw at Millwall in September 1950.

It was midway through the following season before he won a regular place in the Albion side, scoring his first goal for the club in a 5-0 home win over Southend United. Injuries reduced his appearances over the next couple of seasons but in 1954-55 he was back to his best. During the course of that season, the flying winger netted a hat-trick in a 3-1 home win over Watford as Albion finished sixth in the Third Division (South). Injuries again hampered his progress over the following two seasons before in 1957-58 he missed just one game as Brighton won the Third Division (South) Championship.

A more than useful member of the Albion side, he had scored 31 goals in 219 games for the south coast club when he decided to retire at the end of that most successful campaign.

HUNDRED GOALS

Brighton have scored more than 100 League goals in a season on two occasions. The first was in 1955-56 when they finished runners-up to Leyton Orient in the Third Division (South). They scored 112 League goals, more than any other club in the Football League that season. In 1964-65 when they won the Fourth Division Championship, Albion scored 102 goals.

I

INTERNATIONAL PLAYERS

Brighton and Hove Albion's most capped player (ie: caps gained while players were registered with the club) is Steve Penney with 17 caps. The following is a complete list of players who have gained full international honours while with the Seagulls:

ENGLAND		REPUBLIC OF IRELAND	
Tommy Cook	1	John Byrne	1
Steve Foster	3	Tony Grealish	11
Peter Ward	1	Gary Howlett	1
		Joe Kinnear	1
NORTHERN IRELAND		Mark Lawrenson	14
Jack Doran	3	Kieran O'Regan	4
Jimmy Hopkins	1	Michael Robinson	13
Willie Irvine	3	Gerry Ryan	16
Jimmy Magill	5		
Sammy Morgan	2	WALES	
Sammy Nelson	4	Jack Jenkins	8
Steve Penney	17	Peter O'Sullivan	3
Charlie Webb	3	Dean Saunders	5
Danny Wilson	3	Micky Thomas	5

Brighton's first player to be capped was Charlie Webb, who played for Ireland v Scotland on 15 March 1909.

IRVINE, WILLIE

A prolific goal scorer throughout his entire Football League career, Willie Irvine's exploits began in Burnley's Central League side, helping the club to two Championships in 1961-62 and 1962-63. In fact, Irvine made his full international debut for Northern Ireland before he played in the Clarets' League side. Eventually he made his League debut, scoring in a 3-2 win at Arsenal before netting a hat-trick three days later on his home debut against Birmingham City. Developing a prolific partnership with Andy Lochhead, he scored 37 goals in all competitions in 1965-66 but

68

then broke his leg and although he regained full fitness, he was never quite the same again.

He moved to Preston North End but after the Deepdale club were relegated to the Third Division, he joined Brighton and Hove Albion and scored on his debut as the Seagulls beat Fulham 3-2. Irvine quickly formed a useful strike force with Kit Napier and the following season, the pair top-scored with 16 goals each as Brighton finished runners-up to Aston Villa and were promoted to the Second Division.

He scored in each of the opening four games of the 1972-73 season but Albion were relegated as Irvine was unable to weave enough of his magic. He had scored 29 goals in 76 games when he was transferred to his last League club, Halifax Town.

Willie Irvine.
Photo: Lancashire Evening Post

J

JACKSON, JOHN

After a spell managing Loughborough, John Jackson, the former assistant trainer of Wolverhampton Wanderers, returned to training with spells at West Bromwich Albion, Liverpool and Leicester Fosse.

In September 1898, he was appointed manager of Brighton United, the town's original professional club which folded in March 1900 with heavy debts caused by poor crowds and accommodation.

Jackson, who had a chequered time as manager of Brighton, took the revamped club into the Southern League Division One via the Test Match system in 1902-03 after finishing runners-up in the Second Division behind Fulham. Brighton were just beginning to sign a better class of player when Jackson left to concentrate on his public house in the town.

He later returned to the game as manager of Blackpool for a brief spell, although the Seasiders did not appoint an official manager until Bill Norman in 1919.

JENKINS, JACK

Welsh international Jack Jenkins joined Brighton from Pontypridd just prior to the start of the 1922-23 season. The dependable right-back made his Seagulls' debut in the goalless home draw against Norwich City on the opening day of the 1922-23 season. An ever-present in his first season at the Goldstone Ground, he helped Albion finish fourth in the Third Division (South).

Able to play in both full-back positions, Jenkins, a mainstay of the Brighton defence for seven seasons, won the first of his eight international caps for Wales against Northern Ireland in 1924. By 1925-26, he had settled into the left-back position although his progress was hampered the following season by a series of niggling injuries. Having won his last cap against Scotland in October 1926, Jenkins returned to full fitness in

1927-28, taking his tally of games in which he scored four goals to 231 League and Cup appearances before he retired.

JENNINGS, ROY

Full-back Roy Jennings played his first game in Albion colours in a 2-1 home defeat by Watford in January 1953. He was in and out of the side for the next four seasons, only winning a regular first team place towards the end of the 1956-57 season. That campaign saw him take over the mantle as the club's penalty taker, scoring his first in a 2-0 home win over Newport County.

Injuries then hampered his progress and when he returned to first team action midway through the 1958-59 season, he was moved into the centre of Albion's defence, taking over from Ken Whitfield. The move was a huge success and the following season he was ever-present at the heart of the Albion defence. He missed very few games over the next few seasons and was one of few Brighton players to do themselves justice during the relegation season of 1961-62.

Now captain of the club, Jennings could not prevent a second successive relegation in 1962-63 as he finished the season as the club's joint-second top scorer with seven goals. In his last season with the club he reverted to left-back, taking his total appearances in which he scored 22 goals to 297 before retiring.

JENNINGS, SAM

A proven goal scorer with West Ham United, Sam Jennings arrived at the Goldstone Ground towards the end of the 1924-25 season and though he failed to score on his debut against Northampton Town, he netted eight goals in the last 11 games of the season including a hat-trick in a 4-1 home win over Aberdare Athletic.

In 1925-26 Jennings was the club's leading scorer with 20 goals in 41 games as Albion finished fifth in the Third Division (South). He had an even better season in 1926-27, again heading the club's scoring charts with 25 goals in 41 games. His total included four in a 9-3 thrashing of Swindon Town, an amazing scoreline which stood as the club's biggest League win until the 9-1 beating of Newport County in April 1951.

71

The team of 1925 with Sam Jennings (far left in the back row).
Photo: Chris Horlock.

Jennings scored eight goals in the opening 17 games of the 1927-28 campaign, including a hat-trick on the opening day as Brentford were beaten 5-2, before injury curtailed his season. On returning to full fitness, and having scored 63 goals in 115 games for Albion, he joined Nottingham Forest.

JONES, BILLY

Known as 'Bullet', Billy Jones began his career with Birmingham, which he joined from Halesowen in the summer of 1901. After helping the club win promotion to the First Division in 1902-03, he established himself in the Blues' side, forming a good understanding with Benny Green. He was Birmingham's leading scorer for three consecutive seasons, but when Jack Hall forced his way into the side, Jones left to join Brighton and Hove Albion.

After making his debut in a goalless draw at Portsmouth, Jones went on to end the season as the club's leading scorer with 20 goals in 34 games. He would surely have scored more had he not been suspended for two months following a sending-off in the game against Norwich City. Yet despite his absence, Albion went on to win the Southern League Championship. After helping the club win the FA Charity Shield, Jones continued to find the net on a regular basis before in 1912 he returned to St Andrew's.

He was Birmingham's leading scorer in 1912-13 as the Blues finished third in Division Two but at the end of the season, during which he had taken his total of goals to 102 in 252 games, he rejoined Brighton.

Jones, who went on to score 67 goals in 168 games for the Albion, stayed at the Goldstone Ground until the outbreak of the First World War. He played occasionally during the war years before becoming Albion's assistant-trainer, a position he held until 1939.

JUBILEE FUND

The League Benevolent Fund was launched in 1938, fifty years after the start of the Football League, to benefit players who had fallen on hard times. It was decided that the best way to raise funds was for sides to play local 'derby' games with no account being taken of League status.

Brighton played Crystal Palace at Selhurst Park before the start of the 1938-39 season and went down 5-1. The return game at the Goldstone Ground just before the ill-fated 1939-40 season saw the teams share six goals in a most exciting game. It was also the first occasion on which Albion appeared in numbered shirts under the Football League's new directive.

K

KING, ERNIE

Ernie King arrived at the Goldstone Ground from West Bromwich Albion midway through the 1931-32 season, making his debut in a 3-0 defeat at Fulham. It was his only appearance in a Brighton shirt that season but during the early part of the 1932-33 campaign, the strong-tackling full-back won a regular place in the side. Able to play on either flank, he was an important member of the Albion side for the next six seasons.

Midway through the 1937-38 season, his place came under threat from Ernie Marriott and when King was injured in the match against Northampton Town, Marriott took over on merit. This was King's benefit year but because of the serious nature of his injury he was unable to play in his testimonial match against First Division Bolton Wanderers and, having appeared in 217 games for Brighton, was forced to retire.

KIRKWOOD, DAN

Dan Kirkwood was a proven goal scorer with Sheffield Wednesday when he joined Brighton in the close season of 1928. Despite Albion losing 1-0 at Luton Town on his debut Kirkwood ended his first season at the Goldstone Ground as the club's leading scorer with 21 League and Cup goals. This total included him scoring in five consecutive matches and nine in nine matches.

The following season, Kirkwood netted 28 goals as he and Hugh Vallance terrorised the Third Division (South) defences. His total included four goals in the 8-2 win at Merthyr Town and another four in the 6-2 home defeat of Norwich City. He also netted a hat-trick in a 4-3 win over Bournemouth. After Vallance's departure, Kirkwood played up front with Geordie Nicol but found it difficult to hit the target. As the 1931-32 season got underway he found himself partnering Arthur Attwood, but hampered by injuries, Kirkwood, who had scored 82 goals in 181 League and Cup games, left to play for Luton Town.

L

LANE, BILL

Bill Lane was one of the first graduates from Spurs' nursery club at Northfleet when he joined the White Hart Lane staff in the summer of 1924. Unable to hold down a regular place, he moved to Leicester City but was again a frustrated understudy, this time to the prolific Arthur Chandler. Thereafter he spent the rest of his playing career moving rapidly from one club to another. Although he did not stay long with any of his many clubs – Walsall, Reading, Brentford, Watford, Bristol City and Clapton Orient – they all got good value from a player who had the priceless ability to score goals, albeit in the lower reaches of the League. Perhaps the highlight of Bill Lane's career was a three-minute hat-trick for Watford against Clapton Orient in December 1933.

On hanging up his boots, he became assistant-manager of Brentford and after making a brief comeback for Brighton in the war years, became the manager of Guildford City.

In April 1950, Lane moved to Brighton as assistant-manager to Don Welsh. When the former Charlton player left the club in March 1951 to manage Liverpool, Bill Lane took control and steered the Seagulls to fifth place in the Third Division (South) in his first full season.

After three seasons of struggle, Lane resigned, publicly stating that he had done so because of the abolition of the maximum wage, describing it as the most retrogressive step in the history of the game. He then managed Gravesend and Northfleet before scouting for Arsenal and Queen's Park Rangers. He later worked again for Brighton, as a scout in the 1970s.

LANGLEY, JIMMY

After playing as an amateur for Yiewsley, Hayes and Brentford, Jimmy Langley had nine League games as an outside-left for Leeds United. On moving to Brighton and Hove Albion in the summer of 1953, he was converted into a full-back, making his debut for the Seagulls in a 2-1 win at Queen's Park Rangers on the opening day of the 1953-54 season. He was an ever-present in that campaign, his first goal for the club coming in

the final game of the season as Albion completed the double over Queen's Park Rangers, winning 3-1 at the Goldstone Ground.

Langley was appointed Brighton captain for the 1954-55 season and it was not long before he was selected for the England 'B' side against West Germany at Hillsborough. Missing just one game, he skippered Albion to sixth place in the Third Division (South) and at the end of the season went on the FA's summer tour to the West Indies. In 1956 Langley, who had become the club's penalty-taker and won further England 'B' caps, went on tour with the FA team to South Africa.

Jim Langley.
Photo: Lancashire Evening Post.

In February 1957, after scoring 16 goals in 178 games for Brighton, he was transferred to Fulham for £12,000. He was a first team regular for the Craven Cottage club for eight seasons during which he won three full caps and helped the club reach two FA Cup semi-finals and win promotion to the First Division. He had scored 33 goals in 365 games when in July 1965 he was surprisingly allowed to join Queen's Park Rangers. He was a key member of the side that won the League Cup and Third Division Championship and he later left to manage non-League Hillingdon Borough.

LATE FINISHES

Brighton's final match of the season, the play-off final against Notts County at Wembley on 2 June 1991, is so far the latest date for the finish of any Seagulls' season. During the Second World War many curious

76

things occurred, among them the continuance of the 1939-40 season into June. Thus, Brighton's last competitive match in that campaign was on 8 June when they beat Clapton Orient 3-0.

LAWRENSON, MARK

Mark Lawrenson followed his father into the Preston North End side before leaving Deepdale to join Brighton and Hove Albion for a then-record transfer fee of £112,000. The Republic of Ireland international made his League debut in a 1-1 draw with Southampton after playing in two goalless draws against Cambridge United in the League Cup. He had an outstanding first season at the Goldstone Ground, and in 1978-79 Lawrenson, who missed the last three games of the season, helped Brighton finally win promotion to the First Division. He continued to impress, even though after an injury he was moved into midfield. After Albion had two seasons of near-relegation, Lawrenson, who had scored seven goals in 174 games, was allowed to join Liverpool for £900,000.

He quickly slotted into the Reds' defence. Tall, fast and one of the surest tacklers in the game, there were few attackers who ever got the better of him. In 1984 he picked up a European Cup winners' medal and during his years at Anfield also won four League Championship medals, an FA Cup winners' medal and three League Cup winners' medals.

In 1986 injuries began to affect his career and the following season he sustained an Achilles tendon injury which eventually led to his premature retirement. In April 1988 he became manager of Oxford United but after some success he was sacked by the club's owners, the Maxwells, when he questioned the sale of Dean Saunders, a deal done without his knowledge. Nowadays, Mark Lawrenson is a well respected broadcaster.

LDV VANS TROPHY

The LDV Vans Trophy replaced the Autowindscreen Shield for the 2000-01 season. Brighton won their first match in the competition, goals from Johnson and Cullip helping them to a 2-0 victory over Cardiff City. In round two, the Seagulls were held to a 2-2 draw at home after extra time by Brentford, who went on to win the resultant penalty shoot-out 4-2.

In 2001-02, goals from Steele and Lehmann gave Albion a 2-1 win at Swansea City, and Pitcher and Melton helped the club to a similar result against Wycombe Wanderers. In round three, despite Steve Melton getting on the scoresheet, the Seagulls went down 2-1 to Cambridge United.

LEADBETTER, JIMMY

Unable to make much of an impression at Stamford Bridge, Jimmy Leadbetter joined Brighton and Hove Albion as part of the deal that took Johnny McNicol to Chelsea in the summer of 1952.

He made a goal-scoring debut for the Seagulls as they beat Crystal Palace 4-1 on the opening day of the 1952-53 season. Forming a good strike partnership, first with Ken Bennett and then Bert Addinall, Leadbetter netted 10 goals in 34 games in his first season at the Goldstone Ground. In 1953-54, Albion just missed winning the Third Division (South) Championship with Leadbetter again in fine form, scoring 15 goals in 43 games. After one more season with Brighton, in which he was used more in midfield, Leadbetter, who had scored 33 goals in 115 games, left to join Ipswich Town.

An ever-present in the Portman Road club's side in 1958-59, 1959-60 and 1960-61, he played in 138 consecutive League matches between 11 October 1958 and 23 December 1961 and was one of only five players to win Championship medals for all three divisions with the same club.

He went on to score 49 goals in 375 League and Cup games for Ipswich before leaving to play non-League football for Sudbury Town.

LEADING GOAL SCORERS

Brighton and Hove Albion have provided the Football League's divisional leading goalscorer on just three occasions:

1976-77	Peter Ward	Division Three	32 goals
2000-01	Bobby Zamora	Division Three	28 goals
2001-02	Bobby Zamora	Division Two	28 goals

LEAGUE GOALS – CAREER HIGHEST

Tommy Cook holds the Seagulls' record for the most League goals with a career total of 114 goals between 1922 and 1929.

LEAGUE GOALS – LEAST CONCEDED

During the 1922-23 and 1984-85 seasons, the Seagulls conceded just 34 goals in 42 games.

LEAGUE GOALS – MOST INDIVIDUAL

Peter Ward holds the Brighton and Hove Albion record for the most League goals in a season. He scored 32 in the 1976-77 season when the Seagulls finished runners-up in the Third Division.

LEAGUE GOALS – MOST SCORED

Brighton's highest goals tally in the Football League was during the 1955-56 season when they scored 112 goals in finishing as runners-up in the Third Division (South).

LEAGUE VICTORY – HIGHEST

Brighton's best League victories are the 9-1 wins over Newport County on 18 April 1951 and Southend United on 27 November 1965. In the first match Johnny McNicol netted four of the Seagulls' goals and Jack Smith scored a hat-trick in the rout of the Shrimps.

LEEMING, JOE

Joe Leeming joined Brighton and Hove Albion from Bury in the summer of 1908, making his debut in a 3-1 home defeat at the hands of Southampton in the opening game of the 1908-09 season. During the course of that season. Leeming, who was something of a utility defender, wore six different numbered shirts during his 32 appearances.

Joe Leeming was appointed club captain for the 1909-10 season and led the side to the Southern League Championship. An ever-present, he began the season at right-back but following two goalless draws, reverted to left-back, a position he kept for the next six seasons.

He also captained the side to victory over Aston Villa in the FA Charity Shield at Stamford Bridge before injuries restricted his appearances over the next couple of seasons. Once he had regained full fitness, he became the club's best player, his performances being rewarded by selection for a Southern Alliance representative team against the reigning champions, Croydon Common.

Leeming, who appeared in 207 League and Cup games for the Albion, never managed to get his name on the scoresheet.

LITTLE, WALLY

Wally Little, who had played football for the Army during the First World War, joined Brighton at the end of the hostilities and made his Southern League debut in a 3-1 home win over Bristol Rovers. Despite giving an assured performance, the polished left-back had to wait until midway through the season before establishing himself in the Albion side.

Following the club's acceptance into the Football League, he made his first-class debut in Albion's inaugural game in the competition at Southend United. During the course of the following season, Little played at both left-half and inside-left, scoring one of the club's quickest goals in the FA Cup win over Sheffield United.

Little, who became the club's penalty taker, later settled into the side at left-half, his promptings leading to a number of goal scoring chances for Tommy Cook and Jimmy Hopkins. An ever-present in 1924-25, he had his best season in terms of goals scored in 1925-26 when he netted eight times, including two penalties in a match on two occasions – Crystal Palace (Home 3-2) and Bristol Rovers (Home 2-3).

Wally Little scored twenty six times from the spot in his total of 36 goals in 332 games before leaving to play for Clapton Orient where he ended his career.

LLOYD, BARRY

An England youth international, Barry Lloyd began his career with Chelsea but in order to play regular first team football, dropped down a division and joined Fulham. Under Lloyd's captaincy, the Cottagers won promotion to the Second Division. The midfielder also helped Fulham reach the 1975 FA Cup Final but was on the substitute's bench as the Cottagers lost 2-0 to West Ham United. He later played for Hereford United and Brentford, helping the Bees win promotion to the Third Division.

After a spell as manager of Yeovil Town, he took charge of Worthing, helping them from the Isthmian League Second Division to runners-up in the Premier Division in seasons 1983-84 and 1984-85.

In 1986 he joined Brighton as assistant-manager to Alan Mullery, replacing the former England interna-  tional on his departure. The Seagulls were relegated in 1986-87 but Lloyd took them straight back as runners-up to Sunderland in the Third Division. Lloyd kept the same squad and Brighton made a disastrous start to the 1988-89 campaign, losing the first six League games. They recovered sufficiently to finish just outside of the relegation zone.

Again Lloyd spent no money on new players and, as in the previous season, the club finished just outside the danger zone. With Lloyd's youngsters starting to come through, Albion reached the play-offs in 1990-91 but lost to Notts County in the final. The following season was a

Barry Lloyd
Photo: Lancashire Evening Post.

disaster as Albion were relegated. Despite the club's huge debts and the crowd calling for him to be sacked, the board continued to give him their backing until 1993 when he was replaced by Liam Brady.

LONG SERVICE

Charlie Webb was associated with Brighton and Hove Albion as a player and manager from 1908 to 1948. For twenty eight of those years he was the club's manager, by far the longest tenure in Albion's history. Webb made 275 appearances for the club and won three full international caps for Northern Ireland during his time at the Goldstone Ground. He also received a long-service award from the Football League.

Joe Wilson's association with the club was to last thirty eight years as a player, trainer, assistant-manager, caretaker manager and chief scout.

LONGSTAFF, BERT

Long-serving Bert Longstaff made his Brighton debut in a 2-2 draw at Crystal Palace in a top-of-the-ztable United League clash in 1906-07. Towards the end of the following season, he won a regular place in the Seagulls' Southern League side, forming a prolific partnership with Jack Hall and scoring 10 goals in 28 games. On Hall's departure, Longstaff continued to score on a regular basis, teaming up with Martin and helping the club win the Western League. Once again he lost his strike partner and in 1909-10 played up front with 'Bullet' Jones.

Longstaff's total of 14 goals in 39 games included his first hat-trick for the club in a 3-0 home win over Brentford as the Seagulls went on to win the Southern League Championship. He played for Brighton in the FA Charity Shield victory over Aston Villa, after which he was moved out to the wing.

Although his name appeared less frequently on the scoresheet, his accurate crosses created numerous chances for 'Bullet' Jones, Charlie Webb and Jimmy Smith in the seasons leading up to the First World War. He was still the club's first-choice right-winger when the game resumed and made his Football League debut in the first game at Southend United in August 1920. A virtual ever-present in that first season of League football, injuries eventually forced the retirement of one of the club's greatest servants who scored 64 goals in 377 games for the Albion.

LOWEST

The lowest number of goals scored by Brighton and Hove Albion in a single Football League season was 37 in 1986-87. The club's lowest points total in the Football League occurred in 1972-73 when the Seagulls gained just 29 points and finished bottom of the Third Division.

M

MACAULAY, ARCHIE

Archie Macaulay began his football career with Glasgow Rangers, winning Scottish League and Cup winners' medals. In 1937 he was transferred to West Ham United and three years later played for the Hammers in the first wartime Cup Final. He also played in seven Scottish internationals during the war. He had a season playing for Brentford before Arsenal paid £10,000 to secure his services in the summer of 1947. In his first season at Highbury, he won a League Championship medal but in 1953 he moved to Fulham where he ended his playing career.

He went into management with Guildford City and then had a spell as Dundee's trainer-coach before, in April 1957, accepting the post of Norwich City manager. Macaulay took the Canaries from the re-election zone to the semi-finals of the FA Cup in 1959. The following season, City finished as runners-up to Southampton and gained promotion to the Second Division where in their first season they finished fourth.

Macaulay had offers to manage at a higher level and accepted one from West Bromwich Albion. Complaining of not being given a free hand, he left after eighteen months to take over Brighton who were then in the Third Division. He failed to stop them sinking into the Fourth Division soon after he joined the club. However, they were back up as champions of Division Four in 1964-65, scoring 102 goals and gaining 63 points. After a few mediocre seasons, Macaulay – an innovative manager and ahead of his time as a tactician – resigned in October 1968.

MANAGERS

Below is the full list of Brighton and Hove Albion's full-time managers with the dates in which they held office:

John Jackson	1901-1905	Charles Webb	1919-1947
Frank Scott-Walford	1905-1908	Tommy Cook	1947
John Robson	1908-1914	Don Welsh	1947-1951

Bill Lane	1951-1961	Chris Cattlin	1983-1986
George Curtis	1961-1963	Alan Mullery	1986-1987
Archie Macaulay	1963-1968	Barry Lloyd	1987-1993
Fred Goodwin	1968-1970	Liam Brady	1993-1995
Pat Saward	1970-1973	Jimmy Case	1995-1996
Brian Clough	1973-1974	Steve Gritt	1996-1998
Peter Taylor	1974-1976	Brian Horton	1998-1999
Alan Mullery	1976-1981	Jeff Wood	1999
Mike Bailey	1981-1982	Micky Adams	1999-2001
Jimmy Melia	1982-1983	Peter Taylor	2001-2002

MARATHON MATCHES

During the course of the 1969-70 FA Cup competition, Brighton met Walsall in a second round tie that went to four matches. In the first meeting at the Goldstone Ground Brighton's keeper, Geoff Sidebottom, had to be stretchered off with concussion with still almost 30 minutes to play. With Albion leading 1-0, Eddie Spearitt went in goal and performed heroics as the club held out for a 1-1 draw. The replay at Fellows Park also ended all square at 1-1 after extra time with Alex Dawson having scored Brighton's goal in each game. The tie went to a third match, played at neutral Craven Cottage, but after extra time neither side had found the net and the game ended goalless. The fourth meeting at Coventry's Highfield Road ground was nearing full time with the teams again level at 1-1 when Walsall's Colin Taylor netted the winner to separate the teams after seven hours of football.

MARKSMEN – LEAGUE

Brighton's top League goal scorer is Tommy Cook who struck 114 League goals during his eight years at the Goldstone Ground. The leading goal scorers in the Football League are:

Tommy Cook	114	Dan Kirkwood	74	Dennis Foreman	63
Albert Mundy	87	Jimmy Hopkins	72	Dennis Gordon	62
Bert Stephens	86	Ernie Wilson	67	Bobby Zamora	62
Kit Napier	84	Bobby Farrell	66		

MARKSMEN – OVERALL

Tommy Cook is the only Brighton player to have scored more than 100 goals for the club in all competitions. Leading scorers are:

Tommy Cook	123	Dan Kirkwood	82
Kit Napier	99	Jimmy Hopkins	75
Bert Stephens	94	Arthur Attwood	74
Albert Mundy	90	Ernie Wilson	71
Bobby Farrell	83	Dennis Foreman	69

MCNICOL, JOHNNY

Johnny McNicol began his career with Newcastle United but on being unable to break into the Magpies' first team, he joined Brighton for a club record fee of £5,000. He made his Albion debut in a 1-1 home draw against Swindon Town on the opening day of the 1948-49 season, going on to appear in 33 games as the Seagulls finished sixth in the Third Division (South).

In the 1949-50 season, which saw Brighton finish in mid-table, McNicol headed the club's scoring charts with nine goals. He topped the list again the following season, his total of 12 goals including four in the 9-1 rout of Newport County.

By now, McNicol was the finest inside-forward in the lower divisions and it was no surprise that at the end of the 1951-52 season, in which he netted a hat-trick in a 4-1 win at Reading, he was transferred to First Division Chelsea for £12,000 plus Jimmy Leadbetter.

McNicol, who had scored 39 goals in 165 games for Albion, won a League Championship medal with Chelsea in 1954-55 before he gradually moved to wing-half and finally full-back.

After almost six seasons at Stamford Bridge, he joined Crystal Palace where he was immediately made captain. He skippered Palace's first promotion side for 40 years when he took the club out of the Fourth Division in 1960-61. He retired two years later after sustaining a nasty fracture of the cheekbone and a broken jaw.

MELIA, JIMMY

Inside-forward Jimmy Melia began his career with his home club, Liverpool. Unfortunately most of his football was played in the lower

Jimmy Melia.
Photo: Lancashire Evening Post.

Leagues with 1961-62 being his best season as Liverpool took the Second Division title. Life in the top flight was much harder and after a couple of seasons he lost his place and was transferred to Wolverhampton Wanderers for £55,000. His career then took him in numerous directions playing with Wolves, Southampton and Aldershot before trying his hand at management with Crewe and Southport as well as in the Middle East and the United States.

He returned to this country in late 1982 and, after scouting for Brighton, became the club's manager in December 1982. He was only in charge at the Goldstone Ground for nine months but he took the Seagulls to the FA Cup Final in his spell there. Melia resigned as manager when, against his wishes, Chris Cattlin was appointed coach. He later worked in Portugal before having a brief spell as manager of Stockport County.

MELLOR, IAN

Winger Ian Mellor played his early football for Wythenshaw Amateurs before joining Manchester City. Unable to hold down a regular place at Maine Road, he joined Norwich City but after just one season at Carrow Road, he was on his way to the Goldstone Ground.

Mellor scored the only goal of the game on his Brighton debut as the Seagulls beat Crystal Palace on the opening day of the 1974-75 season. After impressing for the first half of the season, Mellor succumbed to a spell of injuries and played little football until the early stages of the following season. He then provided numerous crosses for the likes of Fred Binney, and later in the campaign Peter Ward, and was himself the club's second-highest scorer with nine goals in 33 starts. In 1976-77, when Albion won promotion to the Second Division, Mellor scored 12 goals. Included in his total was a hat-trick in a 7-0 mauling of Walsall. Surprisingly, midway through the following season, he was replaced by new signing Teddy Maybanks and having scored 35 goals in 150 games, was transferred to Chester City.

After impressing at Sealand Road, he was snapped up by Sheffield Wednesday before finally ending his career with Bradford City, where he took his tally of goals for his six League clubs to 66 in 337 League outings.

MOONEY, PAUL

Paul Mooney arrived at the Goldstone Ground from East Stirling and played his first game for the club in a 2-1 home defeat at Queen's Park Rangers in October 1925. That season, although he only made seven appearances, he played at left-back, centre-half and centre-forward. However, the tall, rangy Scot soon settled into the No.5 shirt and began to turn in a series of impressive displays at the heart of the Albion defence. After missing just a couple of games in 1927-28, Mooney began to be troubled by injuries and it was not until 1930-31 that he regained his place in the side. That season he was outstanding, earning himself a deserved benefit match against Notts County, but unfortunately the Seagulls lost 3-1 to the champions elect.

In December 1934, Mooney was involved in a tragic incident in the match against Gillingham, when a clash of heads led to the Kent club's centre-forward, Simeon Raleigh, dying later in the week.

Mooney went on to score 22 goals in 315 games before leaving to play for Vernon Athletic in the Sussex County League.

MOSELEY, GRAHAM

Goalkeeper Graham Moseley began his career as an apprentice with Blackburn Rovers in 1971 but he did not make the first team there and was signed by Derby County a year later. He earned an England youth cap when at the Baseball Ground but spent much of his time as understudy to Colin Boulton. While with Derby, he also had loan spells at Aston Villa and Walsall.

In 1977, Moseley joined Brighton and kept a clean sheet on his debut as Albion beat Bristol Rovers 4-0. In 1978-79, he shared the goalkeeping duties with Eric Steele, keeping nine clean sheets in 17 games as Albion won promotion to the First Division.

Moseley became the club's first-choice keeper in 1979-80, his heroic displays between the posts ensuring that the Seagulls did not make an immediate return to Division Two. Yet the following season he was publicly admonished by manager, Mullery, and replaced by Perry Digweed. Moseley was back to his best in 1981-82 and again in 1982-83 when the club lost its top flight status. He was also in goal when Albion played Manchester United in that season's FA Cup Final.

After playing in just one game the following season, Moseley was ever-present in 1984-85 as Albion finished sixth in Division Two. Keeping 17 clean sheets, he was voted the club's 'Player of the Season'. He was hampered by injuries in the latter stages of his Albion career,and, having played in 224 games for the club, he moved to Cardiff City in what was their first season in the Fourth Division.

MOST MATCHES

Brighton and Hove Albion played their greatest number of matches – a total of 63 – in the 1912-13 campaign. They consisted of 38 Southern League games, three FA Cup games, 16 Southern Alliance games and six Southern Charity Cup games.

MULLERY, ALAN

Alan Mullery began his Football League career with Fulham where his impressive performances in the top flight led to him winning England Under 23 honours. In March 1964, Spurs paid £72,500 to take him to White Hart Lane and two months later he played for the Football League against the Italian League.

The following season he won the first of 35 full caps for England and in 1967 won an FA Cup winners' medal after Spurs had beaten Chelsea.

Appointed club captain, he led Spurs to victory in the 1971 League Cup Final and the 1972 UEFA Cup Final. In the summer of 1972 he returned to Craven Cottage and three years later was elected 'Footballer of the Year' and awarded the MBE. Mullery, who had played in 429 games for Spurs and 412 games for Fulham, then hung up his boots and went into management with Brighton.

In his first season in charge he took the club into the Second Division after finishing as runners-up to Mansfield Town. In 1977-78, Albion challenged strongly for a place in the top flight but ended in fourth place on goal difference from promoted Tottenham Hotspur. However, the following season saw Brighton win promotion to the First Division for the first time in their history after ending the campaign as runners-up to Crystal Palace.

After two seasons of top flight football, Mullery left the Goldstone Ground after refusing to make changes to his coaching staff. He then managed Charlton Athletic but after a year he took charge at Crystal Palace and later Queen's Park Rangers for two years each before finishing his managerial career with another spell at Brighton, from where he was sacked after eight months for alleged lack of commitment.

MUNDY, ALBERT

Inside-forward Albert Mundy began his Football League career with Portsmouth, whom he joined from non-League Gosport Borough. He had scored 12 goals in 51 League outings for Pompey when he left Fratton Park in November 1953 to join Brighton.

He scored on his debut as Albion beat Bristol City 2-1 and ended the season with 11 goals in 21 games as the Seagulls finished the season as runners-up to Ipswich Town. Developing a fine understanding down the right-wing with Dennis Gordon, Mundy was the club's leading scorer in 1954-55 with a total of 18 goals.

He had a magnificent season in 1955-56, netting 28 goals in the club's best total of 112 Third Division (South) goals. Albion again finished as runners-up, this time to Leyton Orient with Mundy netting hat-tricks in the wins over Walsall (Home 3-0) and Bournemouth (Home 4-1). The 1956-57 season saw him heading the scoring charts for a third successive campaign, his total of 20 including another treble in the 8-3 defeat of Reading.

During Albion's Third Division (South) Championship-winning season of 1957-58 Mundy, who had scored 10 goals in 23 games, was surprisingly allowed to leave. The popular forward, who had scored 90 goals in 178 games for Brighton, joined Aldershot where he later ended his first-class career.

MURRAY, BERT

An England schoolboy and youth international, Bert Murray began his League career with Chelsea, where his early performances led to him winning six England Under 23 caps. He helped the club win the League Cup in 1965 but at the end of the following season he left Stamford Bridge to join Birmingham City.

Murray was able to play in a variety of positions. He was an orthodox winger, midfield and right-back, which is where he gave his best performances for the Blues. Not a prolific scorer, he did net a hat-trick in a 3-0 win over Queen's Park Rangers before being transferred to Brighton and Hove Albion in February 1971.

After making his Seagulls' debut in a goalless home draw with Preston North End, he went on to score four goals in 17 games before, in 1971-72, scoring 12 goals in 45 games as Albion won promotion to the Second Division. His consistently good performances won him the 'Player of the Season' award and although he again played well in 1972-73, taking his tally of goals to 26 in 109 games, he left to end his first-class career with Peterborough United.

N

NAPIER, JOHN

John Napier, an Irish schoolboy international began his career with Bolton Wanderers. He progressed quickly as a centre-half, making his League debut against Leyton Orient when he was 18 in the penultimate game of the 1964-65 season. He soon made the position his own and after two appearances for Northern Ireland's Under 23 side, he won his only full international cap against West Germany in May 1966. After losing his place to John Hulme, Napier left Burnden Park to join Brighton and Hove Albion where he became a great favourite.

John Napier.
Photo: Lancashire Evening Post.

He was the club's record signing and made his Albion debut in a 2-1 reversal at Swindon Town on the opening day of the 1967-68 season, going on to miss just one league game in his first season at the Goldstone Ground. An ever-present the following season, he was the first recipient of the club's 'Player of the Season' Award.

Appointed club captain, Napier led Albion to promotion to Division Two in 1971-72 when they were runners-up in the Third Division to Aston Villa. However, in October 1972, after scoring five goals in 247 League and Cup games, he left Albion to play for Bradford City.

He was an ever-present at Valley Parade until being suspended some thirteen months later. In March 1976 Napier went to play for Baltimore in the NASL before returning to become manager of Bradford City in February 1978. Unable to prevent the club's relegation to the Fourth Division, he resigned.

NAPIER, KIT

After failing to make much of an impression with his first two clubs, Blackpool and Preston North End, centre-forward Kit Napier joined Workington. A prolific scorer in the lower divisions, he was signed by Newcastle United's Joe Harvey, hopefully to be developed into a First Division leader who could save the Magpies a hefty fee in the transfer market. Sadly he was not quick enough for top flight football and in September 1966 he joined Brighton.

It was a transaction that proved to be a great piece of business. He scored twice on his debut in a 5-2 defeat of Peterborough United, ending a disappointing season for the club as leading scorer with 10 goals in 32 games.

Napier had a tremendous season in 1967-68, netting 28 League and Cup goals. The following campaign saw him net his first hat-trick in a 3-1 home win over Bristol Rovers. Injuries then began to hamper his progress, although he continued to find the net with great regularity, achieving another treble in a 3-0 win at Mansfield in August 1971.

At the end of that promotion-winning season, Kit Napier, who had scored 99 goals in 291 games for the Seagulls, remained in the Third Division after signing for Blackburn Rovers where he later ended his footballing career.

NEIL, ANDREW

Inside-forward Andrew Neil began his career with his home club, Kilmarnock, before joining Brighton. He played his first game for the Seagulls in a 2-0 defeat at Crystal Palace on Christmas Day 1920. By the start of the following season, he had established himself up front for the south coast club and although he was often outstanding, he did not score enough goals. In 1922-23 he improved his goals tally, netting 10 times in a season in which he was ever-present. Neil continued to pull the strings the following season but towards the end of the campaign, he was transferred to Arsenal for a then club record fee of £3,000.

At Highbury, he played the first roving schemers role for the club – a position later adopted by Alex James. In his first full season with the Gunners, he helped them to the runners-up spot in the First Division before returning to the Goldstone Ground in March 1926.

He took his tally of goals in his two spells to 30 in 185 games before leaving to end his career with Queen's Park Rangers.

NELSON, GARRY

A hardworking striker who can also play on the left side of midfield, Garry Nelson began his career with Southend United, whom he helped win the Fourth Division Championship in 1981-82. He moved to Swindon Town in the summer of 1983 but after two seasons at the County Ground, was on the move again, this time to Plymouth Argyle. It was at Home Park that he began to rediscover his goal-scoring touch and in July 1987, Albion manager Barry Lloyd paid £80,000 to bring him to the Goldstone Ground.

Nelson had an outstanding first season, topping the scoring charts with 32 League and Cup goals. He had scored the only goal of the game on his debut as Brighton beat York City and, although he did not net a hat-trick, he did hit seven doubles. Not surprisingly, Nelson, who was just four goals short of Peter Ward's club record, was named 'Player of the Season'. In 1988-89 he was still the leading scorer with 16 goals. Injuries then hampered his progress and after losing his sharpness in front of goal he was loaned out to Notts County.

Nelson had scored 58 goals in 166 games when in August 1991 he was transferred to Charlton Athletic. He continued to score on a regular basis for the Addicks although towards the end of his stay at The Valley he was recognised more for his literary talents.

In the summer of 1996 he joined Torquay United as player-coach, taking his total of appearances for his seven clubs to 759 before hanging up his boots.

NEUTRAL GROUNDS

Brighton have had to replay a number of FA Cup games on a neutral ground:

Date	Opponents	Venue	Stage	Score
12.02.1906	Middlesbrough	Bramall Lane	Round 2	1-3
20.01.1908	Preston North End	Stamford Bridge	Round 1	1-0
22.01.1923	Corinthians	Stamford Bridge	Round 1	1-0
21.12.1953	Wrexham	Selhurst Park	Round 2	1-3
08.02.1960	Rotherham United	Highbury	Round 4	6-0
15.12.1969	Walsall	Craven Cottage	Round 2	0-0
17.12.1969	Walsall	Highfield Road	Round 2	1-2
06.12.1976	Crystal Palace	Stamford Bridge	Round 1	0-1

Once also in the League Cup

20.09.1977	Oldham Athletic	Filbert Street	Round 2	1-2

The club's other semi-final was played on a neutral ground:

16.04.1983	Sheffield Wednesday	Highbury	Semi-Final	2-1

The club's FA Cup Final appearance in 1983 and play-off Final of 1991, both at Wembley, qualify for inclusion as does the FA Charity Shield of 1910 and the venues of Craven Cottage, Upton Park, The Den and Stamford Bridge which housed the Sussex County Cup matches in the club's early days.

NICKNAMES

The name of the Seagulls for the club is rumoured to have been invented by supporter Lee Phillips in a West Street pub on Christmas Eve 1975 in response to the Crystal Palace chant of 'Eagles, Eagles'. The cry 'Seagulls, Seagulls' soon caught on and in 1977, the club badge was officially changed to a Seagull silhouette.

Many players in the club's history have been fondly known by their nickname. They include:

Tom Higham	1907-1920	'Gunner'
Bill Jones	1909-1912 and 1913-1920	'Bullet'
Ernie Wilson	1922-1936	'Tug'
Oliver Brown	1934-1937	'Buster'
Roy Little	1958-1961	'Doz'

NIGHTINGALE, JACK

Winger Jack Nightingale made his Football League debut for Brighton in a 3-0 win at Exeter City in August 1921, a match in which Jack Doran netted a hat-trick. Halfway through the campaign he began to establish himself as a regular member of the side but he missed much of the following season through injury.

Once he had regained full fitness, he took his place in the team and, although he netted a number of spectacular goals, he was more of a provider, creating chances for Tommy Cook and Jimmy Hopkins. He missed only one game in 1925-26 as Albion finished fifth in the Third Division (South). That season was his best in terms of goals scored as he netted 14 in 41 games including a hat-trick in a 3-0 win at Bournemouth. He went on to score 33 goals in 195 games before leaving the club in the summer of 1927.

NOGAN, KURT

At the end of his first season with Luton Town, Kurt Nogan's potential was recognised by his country when he was awarded a Welsh Under 21 cap against Poland in May 1990. He did his cause no harm with a goal in the 2-0 victory. However, he had to struggle to hold down a regular place at Kenilworth Road and was released at the end of the club's relegation season of 1991-92.

Following a trial period at Peterborough, he joined Brighton in October 1992, making his debut in a 1-0 defeat at Rotherham United. Soon the goals began to flow and he ended the season as the Seagulls' leading scorer with 20 goals in 30 games.

He was Brighton's leading scorer again in 1993-94 with 26 in League and Cup including a hat-trick in a 4-1 home win over Cambridge United. After a bright start to the following season, the goals unaccountably dried up and a shoulder injury then kept him out of the side. Nogan had scored 60 goals in 120 games for the Seagulls when in February 1995 he joined Burnley for a fee of £300,000.

Following a disappointing relegation season, he began to demonstrate his ability as a goal scorer and although he was not as prolific as in his days at the Goldstone Ground, he was highly thought of by Clarets' fans.

In March 1997 he joined Lancashire rivals Preston North End and in his second full season at Deepdale, he scored twice in the televised FA Cup tie against Arsenal and played for Wales 'B'. Injury problems then hampered his progress before he was sold to his home club, Cardiff City, in March 2000 where he spent a frustrating time, failing to start a match in the club's promotion-winning campaign.

NON-LEAGUE

Non-League is the term used for clubs which are not members of the Football League. Brighton's record against non-League opposition in the FA Cup since the Second World War is:

Date	Opponents	Stage	Venue	Score
29.11.1947	Trowbridge	Round 1	Away	1-1
06.12.1947	Trowbridge	Round 1R	Home	5-0
25.11.1950	Tooting and Mitcham	Round 1	Away	3-2
22.11.1950	Yeovil Town	Round 1	Away	4-1
20.11.1954	Tunbridge Wells	Round 1	Home	5-0
09.01.1960	Bath City	Round 3	Away	1-0
13.11.1965	Wisbech Town	Round 1	Home	10-1
04.12.1965	Bedford Town	Round 2	Home	1-1
06.12.1965	Bedford Town	Round 2R	Away	1-2
07.01.1967	Bath City	Round 2	Away	5-0
16.11.1968	Kidderminster Harriers	Round 1	Home	2-2
20.11.1968	Kidderminster Harriers	Round 1R	Away	1-0
05.11.1969	Enfield	Round 1	Home	2-1
21.11.1970	Cheltenham Town	Round 1	Home	4-0
12.12.1970	Hereford United	Round 2	Away	2-1
20.11.1971	Hillingdon Borough	Round 1	Home	7-1
24.11.1973	Walton and Hersham	Round 1	Away	0-0
28.11.1973	Walton and Hersham	Round 1R	Home	0-4
04.01.1975	Leatherhead	Round 3	Home	0-1
07.01.1978	Scarborough	Round 3	Home	3-0
02.01.1982	Barnet	Round 3	Away	0-0
05.01.1982	Barnet	Round 3R	Home	3-1
04.01.1992	Crawley Town	Round 3	Home	5-0
14.11.1992	Hayes	Round 1	Home	2-0

Date	Opponents	Stage	Venue	Score
05.12.1992	Woking	Round 2	Home	1-1
16.12.1992	Woking	Round 2R	Away	2-1
12.11.1994	Kingstonian	Round 1	Away	1-2
12.11.1995	Canvey Island	Round 1	Away	1-1
21.11.1995	Canvey Island	Round 1R	Home	4-1
16.11.1996	Sudbury Town	Round 1	Away	0-0
25.11.1996	Sudbury Town	Round 1R	Home	1-1*
15.11.1997	Hereford United	Round 1	Away	1-2
18.11.2000	Aldershot Town	Round 1	Away	6-2

*Lost 4-3 on penalties.

In 1965-66 the Seagulls cruised to their biggest victory in the competition since thrashing Shoreham 12-0 in the qualifying rounds of 1932-33 when they beat Wisbech Town 10-1 with Charlie Livesey netting a hat-trick.

Probably the worst FA Cup defeat came in 1973-74 when Brighton were beaten 4-0 at the Goldstone Ground by Walton and Hersham, the Amateur Cup holders. The club were humiliated again the following season when Chris Kelly, the 'Leatherhead Lip', scored the only goal of the game.

O

OLDEST PLAYER

The oldest player to line-up in a Brighton first team is Jimmy Case. He was 41 years 165 days old when he played his last game for the club against Swansea City (Home 0-2) on 31 October 1995.

O'SULLIVAN, PETER

Welsh international Peter O'Sullivan began his career with Manchester United but on being unable to make much headway at Old Trafford, joined Brighton in the summer of 1970. O'Sullivan, who was Fred Goodwin's last signing, made his Albion debut in the goalless home draw against Torquay United on the opening day of the 1970-71 season. After a few indifferent displays in the early part of the campaign, he settled down to become one of the club's most consistent performers.

In 1971-72, when Albion won promotion to the Second Division, O'Sullivan was ever-present and scored 12 goals from his position on the left-wing. He was also ever-present in 1973-74, appearing in 176 consecutive League games before an injury at Charlton Athletic in September 1974 ended the run. O'Sullivan was ever-present again in 1975-76 as Albion just missed out on promotion back to Division Two and had an outstanding season in 1976-77 as the Seagulls finally returned to the Second Division as runners-up to Mansfield Town.

Peter O'Sullivan.

98

In 1977-78, he was named as the club's 'Player of the Season' and the following season, his midfield creativity provided a number of goal scoring opportunities for Maybank and Poskett as the Seagulls finally won promotion to the First Division.

O'Sullivan continued to be one of the club's best players for a further two seasons of top flight football but after scoring 43 goals in 491 games he left the Goldstone Ground to play for Fulham.

After one season with the Cottagers, he lost his place in the startling line-up and after loan spells with Charlton Athletic and Reading, he tried his luck in Hong Kong before ending his career with Aldershot.

OVERSEAS PLAYERS

Israeli international Moshe Gariani joined the Seagulls from Macabbi Netanya in the summer of 1980 but made just one substitute appearance before returning to his homeland.

Dutch triallist Hans Kraay arrived at the Goldstone Ground from NAC Breda, the subject of a lengthy ban in his home country. The midfielder won a regular place in the Brighton side midway through the 1984-85 season, scoring three goals in 23 games before being released.

United States international goalkeepers, Tony Meola and Jurgen Sommer, have both kept goal for the Seagulls in one League match – Meola in a 1-1 draw with Wolverhampton Wanderers and Sommer in a goalless draw at Cambridge United.

Sergei Gotsmanov arrived at the Goldstone Ground from Dynamo Minsk in February 1990. A Russian international, he scored on his full debut in a 1-1 home draw against Oldham Athletic. Impressing with his skill and pace, he scored four goals in 16 League games before joining Southampton. Another Russian international, Igor Gurinovich, joined the Seagulls during the course of the 1990-91 season and scored in a 2-1 defeat by Notts County, one of four League appearances.

Rumanian defender, Stefan Iovan, joined Brighton in March 1991 and he appeared in all of the club's play-off matches at the end of the season.

Nigerian international, David Adekola, joined the Seagulls from Cambridge United in October 1996 but suffered a knee injury on his debut and was substituted. He was later released at the end of his trial period.

Icelandic midfielder, Valur Gislason, joined the Seagulls on loan from Arsenal after failing to get a game at Highbury. He struggled to shine and after Brighton failed to win in any of his seven consecutive matches, he was transferred to Norwegian club, Stromsgodset.

Albion's second Nigerian international, Emeka Ifejiagwa, joined the club on loan from Charlton Athletic and scored the only goal of the game on his debut against Barnet. A giant of a centre-half, work permit problems caused his loan spell to be cut short.

Italian striker, Lorenzo Pinamonte, had a loan spell with the Seagulls during the 1999-2000 season, scoring twice against Exeter City before returning to Bristol City who sold him on to Brentford.

Former Dutch marine, Michel Kuipers, bought himself out of the armed services to pursue a career in football and after playing for SDW Amsterdam had one match in goal for Bristol Rovers before joining Brighton and helping them win the Third and Second Division Championships in successive seasons.

P

PENALTIES

During the club's early years in the Football League, their 'penalty king' was Wally Little who converted 26 in League and Cup matches. One of these came in the 5-0 win over Queen's Park Rangers on 28 March 1925, a match set aside for his benefit after five years outstanding service.

On 8 March 1952, Brighton beat Walsall 5-1 in a Third Division (South) game. Three minutes from time, Jackie Mansell, who had scored from a penalty in the first-half, waived his second penalty to allow Brighton inside-left Ken Bennett to complete his hat-trick. But Bennett's shot was parried by Walsall goalkeeper Jack Lewis, only for Mansell to follow up and score.

The most penalties ever awarded in a single match in British football is five, in a remarkable match between Crystal Palace and Brighton at Selhurst Park on 27 March 1989. All five came in a 27 minute spell either side of half-time. Palace were awarded four of the five kicks (one scored, three missed) by referee Kelvin Morton and Brighton got one (scored by Alan Curbishley). The match finished 2-1 to Palace.

PENNEY, STEVE

Winger Steve Penney was playing for his home club Ballymena United when he was spotted by Brighton who signed him in November 1983. He immediately won a place in Albion's Second Division side, making his League debut in a 3-1 defeat at Barnsley.

He scored his first senior goal in English football in Albion's impressive 3-1 win at Derby in March 1984 but in the main, his role was out wide providing crosses for his colleagues in the middle. So successful was he that, less than a year after crossing the water, Steve Penney made his full international debut in Northern Ireland's 3-0 victory over Israel in October 1984. He went on to collect 17 full caps for his country including games against Algeria and Spain in the 1986 World Cup Finals in Mexico.

He played in Brighton's side relegated to Division Three in 1987, but in 1989 began the knee problems that were to plague him for more than two years. After scoring 15 goals in 162 games, he was released by Brighton and joined Scottish Premier League club, Hearts. He joined Burnley on a free transfer in the summer of 1992. Sadly he continued to be dogged by injury and announced his retirement two years later.

PIPER, STEVE

Central defender Steve Piper made his debut for his home club during Brighton's relegation season of 1972-73 as the Seagulls went down 1-0 at home to eventual champions Burnley. Occupying a variety of defensive positions over the next couple of seasons, Piper was an important member of the Albion side that just missed out on promotion to the Second Division in 1975-76. The following season, he was ever-present as the club won promotion to Division Two as runners-up to Mansfield Town.

Wearing the No.10 shirt, his total of four goals included the winner in the 3-2 defeat of Sheffield Wednesday that clinched promotion for the Seagulls. Midway through the 1977-78 season, with Albion pushing for promotion to the top flight, Piper, who had scored nine goals mainly from set pieces in 190 games, left to join Portsmouth.

PITCH

The Withdean Stadium pitch measures 110 yards by 70 yards.

PLASTIC

Four league clubs replaced their normal grass playing pitches with artificial surfaces at one stage or another. Queen's Park Rangers were the first in 1981 but the Loftus Road plastic was discarded in 1988 in favour of a return to turf. Luton Town (1985) Oldham Athletic (1986) and Preston North End (1986) followed.

The Seagulls never played on the Loftus Road or Kenilworth Road plastics and only once at Deepdale where they went down 3-0 during the

1987-88 season. Brighton played Oldham Athletic on their Boundary Park plastic five times, drawing two and losing three. The club's worst result against the Latics came in their last meeting on 1 December 1990 when they were beaten 6-1 as Oldham went on to win the Second Division Championship.

PLAY-OFFS

Brighton's only appearance in the play-offs came at the end of the 1990-91 season in which they finished sixth in Division Two. Their opponents in the two-legged semi-final were Millwall. The first leg at the Goldstone Ground saw the Lions take the lead after 14 minutes but Albion equalised through Mark Barham just before the interval. The outcome was settled in the space of seven incredible second-half minutes as Mike Small put Albion ahead in the 53rd minute, set up Clive Walker for the third two minutes later and then laid on the chance for Robert Codner to make it 4-1 in the 59th minute.

In the second leg at The Den, the Lions again went ahead but two second-half strikes from Codner and Robinson gave Albion a 2-1 win on the night and a magnificent 6-2 aggregate victory.

Albion's opponents in the Wembley play-off final were Notts County, who had finished fourth in Division two, ten points ahead of Brighton. A crowd of 59,940 saw Albion dominate the early proceedings but it was Notts County who took the lead after 29 minutes. Just before half-time, Clive Walker headed against the County crossbar with keeper Steve Cherry well beaten. Early in the second-half, Dean Wilkins curled a free kick against the crossbar but it was Tommy Johnson who scored his and County's second goal on the hour mark. County extended their lead after 71 minutes through Dave Regis before Dean Wilkins netted a consolation goal in the last minute of the game.

POINTS

Under the three points for a win system which was introduced in 1981-82, Brighton's best points tally was 92 points in 2000-01 when they won the Third Division Championship. Their best points haul under the former two points for a win system was 65 in 1955-56 when they were runners-up in the Third Division (South) and 1971-72 when they again finished runners-up in Division Three.

Brighton's worst record under either system was the meagre 29 points secured in 1972-73 when they finished bottom of the Second Division and were relegated.

POOLS WAR

Littlewoods Pools had been in operation since February 1923 and a number of companies had followed suit. However, midway through the 1935-36 season, the Football League management committee objected to the use of its fixtures for the purposes of gambling and so in an attempt to thwart the pools companies, for two Saturdays, the published fixtures were scrapped and replaced by other matches.

The clubs were given very short notice as to who their opponents would be. On 29 February 1936 a visit to Notts County turned out to be a trip to Gillingham (Won 2-1) and the following Saturday, Cardiff City (Won 1-0) visited the Goldstone Ground instead of Bristol Rovers. Not surprisingly, attendances were down, an emphatic defeat for the Football League. Thankfully normal service was soon resumed both on the pitch and on the pools' coupons.

POSTPONED

The bleak winter of 1962-63 proved to be one of the most chaotic seasons in British soccer. The worst Saturday for League action in that awful winter was 2 February 1963 when only four Football League fixtures went ahead. One of these was at the Goldstone Ground where visitors Halifax Town won by the only goal of the game. The worst Saturday for the FA Cup was 5 January 1963, the day of the third round, when only three of the 32 ties could be played. Unfortunately, Albion had been knocked out of the competition at the first round stage by Southend United.

On 31 October 1954, Brighton's home game against Queen's Park Rangers was postponed so as to avoid a clash with the All Blacks game of Rugby Union against the Southern Counties at the nearby greyhound stadium.

POWNEY, BRIAN

Goalkeeper Brian Powney was just 17 when he made his Brighton debut on the final day of the club's relegation season of 1961-62, in a 2-0 defeat at Derby County. The club suffered a second successive relegation the following season with Powney making just eight appearances.

It was midway through the 1963-64 season before Powney established himself as the club's first-choice keeper and the following season he missed only a handful of games as Albion won the Fourth Division Championship. After that, he was a virtual ever-present for the next nine seasons, only missing games through injury.

In 1971-72 he was in outstanding form, keeping 14 clean sheets as Albion won promotion to the Second Division as runners-up to Aston Villa. Despite some heroic performances between the posts the following season he could not prevent the Seagulls being relegated and after one more season at the Goldstone Ground, Powney, who made 368 appearances, left the club.

PROMOTION

Brighton have been promoted on eight occasions. After being admitted to the Football League in 1920-21, Albion had to wait until 1957-58 before winning their first promotion as champions of the Third Division (South). The club then suffered two relegations before winning the Fourth Division Championship in 1964-65. After seven seasons of Third Division football, the Seagulls won promotion to the Second Division in 1971-72 as runners-up to Aston Villa. The club ended the season with eight wins and four draws in their last 12 games. After only one season in Division Two, Brighton were relegated but won their fourth promotion in 1976-77 as runners-up in the Third Division to Mansfield Town. It was a campaign in which Peter Ward broke the club scoring record with 36 goals – 32 in the League. In fact, Ward was the leading scorer in the entire Football League.

A couple of seasons later, Albion had won promotion to the First Division in one of the most closely fought campaigns. Having lost just one of their last 16 League games, the Seagulls finished on 56 points, one behind champions Crystal Palace and the same as Stoke City. Sunderland finished one point behind Albion and just missed out on promotion.

Eight years and two relegations later, Brighton found themselves back in the Third Division but after just one season, they won promotion as runners-up to Sunderland. The Seagulls won seven and drew three of their last ten games to pip Walsall for the second promotion place.

In 2000-01, Albion won the Third Division Championship, finishing ten points clear of second placed Cardiff City. Last season, the club not only achieved its eighth promotion but also its second successive divisional championship in winning the Division Two title.

Q

QUICKEST GOAL

There may have been quicker goals scored for Brighton and Hove Albion in its hundred plus years of existence, but they do not appear in the records.

The one that does was netted by Peter Ward during the course of the 1976-77 season when he topped the club's charts with a total of 36 League and Cup goals.

His strike in the 1-1 League Cup fourth round draw with First Division Derby County came after just 37 seconds.

R

RAPID SCORING

In the final game of the club's Third Division (South) Championship winning season of 1957-58, Brighton entertained Watford, knowing that they needed a win to clinch the title. Playing in only his seventh league game was 20-year-old local boy Adrian Thorne. He had just been demobbed from National Service with the Army. The game was only five minutes old when Thorne put Albion in front and three minutes later, he made it 2-0. Within sixty seconds he had completed his hat-trick – three goals in the space of four minutes. Shortly afterwards, Glen Wilson scored from the penalty-spot and Thorne netted his fourth to give Albion a 5-0 lead at the interval. Watford played with a bit more purpose in the second-half but Thorne netted his fifth and Albion's sixth a minute from time.

RECEIPTS

Record receipts were £109,615 for the FA Cup third round match against non-League Crawley Town at the Goldstone Ground on 4 January 1992.

REED, BILLY

Rhondda-born winger Billy Reed played his early football with his home club before joining Cardiff City. Unable to make the grade at Ninian Park, the former Welsh amateur moved to Brighton and Hove Albion in the summer of 1948 but had to wait until Christmas Day before making his league debut in a 1-1 draw at Exeter City.

Reed found himself in and out of the Brighton side over the next couple of seasons but in 1951-52 he was not only ever-present but the club's top scorer with 19 goals, a total which included a hat-trick in a 5-1 win over Ipswich Town. Reed was leading the club's scoring charts again the following season when he was transferred to Ipswich, having scored 37 goals in 132 games for the Seagulls.

At Portman Road he was considered the best right-winger in the Third

Division. Possessing exceptional dribbling skill, he helped the Suffolk club win the Third Division (South) Championship. Although Town were relegated in 1954-55, Reed was one of Ipswich's best players, netting a hat-trick in a 5-2 win over Walsall. It was during that campaign that he was capped twice by Wales and in the process became the first player to receive full international honours while on Ipswich's books. He won another Third Division (South) Championship medal in 1956-57 but then left to end his career with Swansea Town.

RE-ELECTION

Brighton went to Swansea Town for the last match of the 1947-48 season, needing a win to avoid having to apply for re-election to the Third Division (South). Swansea were awarded a penalty and Dai James who had never missed from the spot, came up to take it. Harry Baldwin the Brighton goalkeeper had saved the last four penalties against him and he made it five with a full length dive in which he caught the ball with both hands. He succeeded in keeping a clean sheet that day but Brighton could only draw 0-0 and had to go cap in hand to the League.

RELEGATION

The Seagulls have been relegated on seven occasions. The first time was in 1961-62 when, after four seasons of Second Division football, they finished bottom of the table. The following season, after a run of 11 League games without victory, they found themselves bottom of the Third Division. By the end of the campaign, they were still in the bottom four and relegated to the Fourth Division for the first time in their history.

There followed a couple of promotions before Albion's third relegation in 1972-73 when their second taste of Division Two football proved a disaster. After drawing 2-2 at Cardiff City on 4 November, they lost 12 consecutive league matches before beating Luton Town 2-0. Not surprisingly they finished bottom of the League.

Two promotions followed and in 1979-80, the Seagulls were in the First Division. After four seasons of top flight football, they were relegated, finishing bottom of the First Division, eight points from safety. It was even more disappointing as that season they had reached the FA Cup Final.

The Seagulls were relegated for a fifth time in 1986-87 after four seasons in the Second Division, winning only two of their last 20 matches. Then, after one season of Third Division football, Brighton won promotion, only to be relegated in 1991-92.

The club's last experience of relegation was in 1995-96 when it took seven games for Albion to notch up their first win. The biggest handicap was the team's failure to pick up points at home consistently and they only once managed two consecutive wins.

RITCHIE, ANDY

Andy Ritchie began his career with Manchester United and looked like having a big future at Old Trafford but in October 1980 he was surprisingly sold to Brighton and Hove Albion for £500,000.

He made his Albion debut in a 4-1 defeat at Aston Villa but formed a useful strike partnership with Michael Robinson that just kept the Seagulls in the top flight. During the early stages of the 1981-82 season, Ritchie came in for a bit of criticism from the Albion fans but after netting twice in the 4-1 defeat of Manchester City, he found his form and ended the season as the club's leading scorer with 13 goals. Albion finished in mid-table and Ritchie was voted 'Player of the Season'.

Injuries hampered his progress in 1982-83 when Albion were relegated but it was still a surprise when in March of that season he was swapped for Leeds United's Terry Connor. Ritchie, who had scored 26 goals in 102 games, spent much of his time at Elland Road in a dispute over his contract, later moved to Oldham Athletic.

He proved a bargain buy, scoring a stack of goals for the Latics and helping them reach the League Cup Final and FA Cup semi-final in 1990 and win the Championship of the old Second Division in 1991. Then after struggling with injuries, he joined Scarborough before returning to Boundary Park as the club's manager.

ROBINSON, MICHAEL

All-action striker Michael Robinson began his Football League career with Preston North End but in July 1979 after just 45 league appearances for the Deepdale club, Manchester City paid Preston a staggering

£750,000 for the promising youngster. He never seemed to make the grade at Maine Road and a year later he was sold to Brighton for half the price.

He made his Seagulls' debut in a 2-0 home win over Wolverhampton Wanderers on the opening day of the 1980-81 season, going on to end the campaign in which Albion just avoided relegation, as the club's leading scorer with 19 goals. Not surprisingly he was named 'Player of the Season'.

Michael Robinson.
Photo: Lancashire Evening Post.

In 1981-82 he teamed up with Andy Ritchie and although his goals tally fell, the Republic of Ireland international continued to be one of the best strikers in the top flight. Sadly, following Albion's relegation to the Second Division in 1982-83, Robinson, who had scored 43 goals in 133 games, left to join Liverpool.

A little over a year later, he was sold to Queen's Park Rangers. He later played for Osasuna in the Spanish League and now enjoys a successful career as a commentator with Spanish television.

ROBSON, JOHN

John Robson was Middlesbrough's first secretary and in 1899 following the club's acceptance into the Football League, he became its first manager. In 1901-02 he led the club to promotion to the First Division, Boro finishing runners-up to West Bromwich Albion. When there was a scandal over irregular payments in 1905, Robson was absolved of any responsibility but still vacated the post to take charge of Crystal Palace as the club's first manager. He led Palace to the Southern League Second Division Championship at their first attempt before in March 1908 taking over the reins at Brighton.

There he drove the players hard but looked after their welfare and recreational activities. In 1909-10 he led Albion to the Southern League Championship with 59 points, conceding only 29 goals, and they surprisingly beat First Division Aston Villa 1-0 in the FA Charity Shield match . The following season, Brighton finished third in the Southern League and although they were always in the top half of the table, they never challenged seriously for the title. In December 1914, Robson was released to take over as manager of Manchester United and presented with a silver rose-bowl in appreciation of his seven years at the Goldstone Ground.

At Old Trafford he later took over the duties of secretary but ill-health led to him stepping down to assistant secretary. Shortly after the end of his fifth year in this post he died of pneumonia.

RUNNERS-UP

Brighton and Hove Albion have been runners-up in a division of the Football League on six occasions:

1953-54 (Third Division South)	1976-77 (Third Division)
1955-56 (Third Division South)	1978-79 (Second Division)
1971-72 (Third Division)	1987-88 (Third Division).

RYAN, GERRY

Republic of Ireland international winger Gerry Ryan was playing for his home club of Bohemians when Derby County manager Tommy Docherty paid £50,000 for his services in September 1977. Ryan settled in well but after just one season he was transferred to Brighton for £80,000.

He made his Seagulls' debut in a 2-2 draw at Stoke City, going on to score 10 goals and help the club win promotion to the First Division as runners-up to Crystal Palace. Ryan was an important member of Albion's top flight side, although injuries ruled him out for most of the 1980-81 campaign. He was substitute for Albion in the 1983 FA Cup Final with Manchester United, coming on for Chris Ramsey in the drawn game and for Gary Howlett in the 4-0 defeat.

On 2 April 1985, Gerry Ryan played the last of his 199 games in which he scored 39 goals for Brighton against Crystal Palace. During the match he broke his leg and the injury was so serious that it brought an abrupt and premature end to his League career.

S

SAUNDERS, DEAN

Dean Saunders made his Football League debut for his home club, Swansea City, but was not highly thought of by manager John Bond.

Dean Saunders.
Photo: Lancashire Evening Post.

Following a loan spell at Cardiff City, Saunders signed for Brighton and Hove Albion in the summer of 1985.

He made his debut as a substitute for Chris Hutchings in a 2-2 home draw against Grimsby Town on the opening day of the 1985-86 season, finishing the campaign as the club's leading scorer with 19 goals. His form was such that he won the first of seventy five full international caps for Wales when he played against the Republic of Ireland. Not surprisingly he was voted the club's 'Player of the Season'.

With Albion heading towards the Third Division Saunders, who had scored 26 goals in 86 games, was transferred to Oxford United for just £60,000 to raise cash. When Oxford were relegated to the Second Division, he was sold to Derby County. After three seasons as the Rams' leading scorer, he was sold to Liverpool for £2.9 million, a record transfer fee between two English clubs.

Despite finishing as leading scorer in all competitions and collecting an FA Cup winners' medal, he was sold to Aston Villa for £2.3 million. As at Derby, he was leading scorer for three consecutive seasons before leaving to play for Turkish club, Galatasaray. He returned to the Premiership with Nottingham Forest before joining Sheffield United on a free transfer.

The Yorkshire club were powerless to prevent his £500,000 move to Benfica in December 1998. The much-travelled striker returned to these shores in the summer of 1999 to play for Bradford City but after a couple of seasons at Valley Parade it was decided not to renew his contract.

SAWARD, PAT

Born in County Cork, Pat Saward was raised in South London and turned out for Crystal Palace on amateur forms as a youngster. However, it was with Millwall that he began his Football League career. A tall, well-built and talented left-half, he suffered from barracking from parts of the crowd at The Den and in August 1955, he joined Aston Villa for £16,000.

In six seasons at Villa Park he made 152 League appearances and won an FA Cup winners' medal in 1957 as well as captaining the club to the Second Division Championship in 1959-60, following their relegation the previous season. In March 1961 he was transferred to Huddersfield Town before later joining Coventry City as their coach.

In the summer of 1970, Saward was appointed manager of Brighton and Hove Albion. He helped the club win promotion to Division Two in 1971-72 as runners-up to Aston Villa but the club really needed a number of new signings to boost an average squad and the Seagulls were instantly relegated. His sides played attacking football but after a poor start to the 1973-74 season, he was sacked by the board which felt that he could no longer motivate the side. He later coached the Saudi Arabian club AL-NASR and then ran a holiday business in Minorca.

SCOTT-WALFORD, FRANK

Frank Scott-Walford was an amateur on Tottenham's books before joining Isthmian League club, London Caledonians. But his playing ability never matched his organisational skill and he went on to form the Enfield and District League and became a Southern League referee.

In March 1905, Scott-Walford became Brighton's manager but within two months all but three of his playing staff had departed, leaving him with the awesome task of piecing together a new squad before the start of the next season. He managed to get a team together but an FA Council meeting on 2 April 1906 reported that he was mainly responsible for irregularities in approaching other clubs' players before their contracts had expired and he was suspended from management until the end of July. Despite the ban, a number of clubs were interested in having him as their manager but Scott-Walford still had two years of his contract to run with Brighton.

Negotiations were protracted and it was March 1908 when Albion found John Robson and Scott-Walford was allowed to leave and take charge of Leeds City. He took a number of his Brighton players with him to Elland Road but both they and he failed to make an impression and at the end of the 1911-12 season, the club had to seek re-election.

Not surprisingly Scott-Walford stepped down. He later managed Coventry, many of whose matches in the Second Division of the Southern League were in South Wales with the result that the club made a huge loss due to the increased travelling costs. He managed to keep the club going until 1915 when business was wound up.

SECOND DIVISION

Brighton have had seven spells in the Second Division. They were promoted in 1957-58 as champions of the Third Division (South), but four seasons later they were relegated. Four of the club's spells in the Second Division have, in fact, lasted for four seasons, although their next in 1972-73 lasted just one season and they were again relegated to the Third Division.

In 1978-79, Albion ended their third spell of two seasons in the Second Division with promotion to the top flight, as runners-up to Crystal Palace. After four seasons of First Division football, which ended with their relegation in 1982-83, the Seagulls embarked on a fourth spell in Division Two. A disastrous campaign in 1986-87 saw them finish bottom of the table but after one season of Third Division football, they won promotion to start their fifth spell in 1988-89.

Four seasons later, Albion finished in the bottom three but because of reorganisation, they started the 1992-93 season in the 'new' Second Division. Another spell of four seasons ended with the club being relegated to the Third Division.

After winning the Division Three Championship in 2000-01, the Seagulls began their seventh spell in the Second Division last season but after winning their second successive divisional title, will start the 2002-03 campaign in Division One.

SEXTON, DAVE

The son of a Southern Area middleweight boxing champion, Dave Sexton played his early football with Chelmsford City before moving on to Luton Town. Unable to make much of an impression, he joined West Ham United, for whom he scored some valuable goals. In May 1956 he moved to Orient and from there to Brighton and Hove Albion, making his Seagulls' debut at Aldershot and scoring in a 3-2 win. That season, Sexton scored 18 goals in 26 games as Albion won the Third Division (South) Championship. Included in his total were hat-tricks in the wins over Crystal Palace (Away 4-2) and Gillingham (Home 5-2).

Injuries hampered his progress the following season and in May 1959 after scoring 28 goals in 53 games, he joined Crystal Palace. Sadly a knee injury ended his career.

As a manager, he helped Chelsea to the FA Cup Final of 1970 and the European Cup Winners' Cup Final of 1971. He led his next two clubs, Queen's Park Rangers and Manchester United to the runners-up spot in the First Division as he had with Chelsea. Although he was dismissed as manager of Coventry City, he was appointed assistant to England manager Bobby Robson in 1983. He was later put in charge of the new Soccer School and the England Under 21 squad.

SHERPA VAN TROPHY

This competition for associate members of the Football League was first sponsored by Sherpa Van in the 1987-88 season. Brighton's first match in the Sherpa Van Trophy saw them thrash Fulham 6-1 at Craven Cottage with Kevin Bremner and Garry Nelson scoring a couple of goals each. Both of those players were on target again in the second group game as Southend United were beaten 3-2. The Shrimpers were also Brighton's opponents in the first round proper of the competition and Bremner and Nelson continued to hit the target in a 4-2 victory. A goal from Gerry Armstrong gave Brighton a 1-0 victory over Hereford United to set up a southern area semi-final clash with promotion rivals Notts County. A win would have taken the Seagulls to within 90 minutes of the Wembley Final but County took Brighton apart, winning 5-1 in front of a Goldstone Ground crowd of 8,499.

SIMOD CUP

The Simod Cup replaced the Full Members' Cup for the 1987-88 season but it was in 1988-89, following the club's promotion to the Second Division, before Brighton participated in the competition. In what proved to be the club's only match in the Simod Cup, Garry Nelson scored for the Seagulls in a 3-1 defeat at Bradford City.

SMITH, GORDON

Scottish Under 21 international Gordon Smith joined the Seagulls from Glasgow Rangers in the summer of 1980 and made his Football League debut in the opening game of the 1980-81 season, scoring in a 2-0 win over Wolves. The ball-playing midfielder went on to score 10 goals in 38 games including a 19-minute hat-trick that secured a point in a 3-3 draw at Coventry City. After a disappointing 1981-82 season, Smith was back to his best the following campaign. Despite his midfield promptings, Albion lost their top flight status.

Smith was a member of the Brighton side that played Manchester United in the 1983 FA Cup Final at Wembley. He scored the game's opening goal after 13 minutes but in extra time he was guilty of missing the chance that would most surely have given Albion the Cup. Ten yards out and completely unmarked, Smith took Robinson's pass but his shot struck the legs of the oncoming Gary Bailey who then dived on the ball to prevent the Scot getting to the rebound.

In March 1984, Smith, who had scored 25 goals in 125 first team out-ings, left to play for Manchester City before moving to Oldham Athletic where he ended his league career.

SMITH, JACK

Jack Smith began his career with his home club, Hartlepool United, scoring 49 goals in 119 league games before being transferred to Watford. Unable to make much of an impression at Vicarage Road, he moved on to Swindon Town where he rediscovered his scoring form. After a couple of impressive seasons at the County ground, Smith left to join Brighton midway through the 1963-64 campaign.

It was in the following season that he made his name. Playing alongside his namesake, Bobby, he scored 17 goals in 35 games as Albion won the Fourth Division Championship. In 1965-66, Albion finished mid-table in the Third Division but beat Southend United 9-1 with Jack Smith hitting a second-half hat-trick.

During the early part of the next campaign, Smith, who had scored 36 goals in 96 League and Cup games, left to play for Notts County, where he later ended his first-class career.

SMITH, POTTER

Inside-forward Potter Smith arrived at the Goldstone Ground from Cardiff City and made his Brighton debut in a 1-0 defeat at Bristol Rovers on the opening day of the 1929-30 season. He netted both goals on his home debut as Albion beat Watford 2-1 and his promptings created a wealth of scoring opportunities for Brighton forwards with Arthur Attwood netting 25 goals in 27 games in 1931-32 and 20 goals in 1932-33.

Smith had missed a few games when an injury sustained at Northampton Town on Boxing Day 1933 forced him out of most of the season's remaining games. He was back to full fitness in 1934-35 when he had his best season in terms of goals scored with nine in 36 outings.

The following campaign saw Potter Smith take over the captaincy of the club which finished seventh in the Third Division (South). In 1936-37 he was badly injured in the opening match at Gillingham but returned two months later to lead the Seagulls to third place.

At the end of that season, Smith, who had been plagued by injury, decided to retire, having scored 57 goals in 320 games for Albion.

SOUTHERN LEAGUE

Brighton United were elected straight into the First Division of the Southern League for the 1898-99 season. They were the first professional club in the town but soon folded and were wound up in March 1900.

United played home games at the north end of the Sussex County Cricket ground at Eaton Road, Hove but were barred from the first and last months of the season as the cricket club required the pitch. In 1899-1900 United lasted just 22 games, gaining nine points and suffering some heavy defeats. There was no cover at the County ground and the weather always seemed to be terrible when they were at home.

In 1901-02, Brighton and Hove Rangers joined the Second Division of the Southern League. Formed in 1900 out of the ashes of Brighton United, Rangers played their first season at North End Rangers' ground at Withdean. They moved to the County Ground on joining the Southern League and changed their name to Brighton and Hove Albion in the close season of 1901. Their first season in the Southern League Division Two was a successful one, with them finishing third – just out of the two pro-motion places.

In 1902-03, only six clubs were to contest the Second Division. Brighton and Fulham ended the season on the same points and as goal average did not count, a play-off was expected to take place, but it did not. Promotion was not automatic and 'Test Matches' between the bottom two clubs of the First Division and the top two from the Second Division took place. Brighton's opponents were Watford who were beaten 5-3 with Ben Garfield scoring four of the club's goals.

Sadly, in 1903-04 the team struggled all season and finished one place off the bottom of the table. Bottom placed Kettering Town withdrew from the Southern League and Watford were promoted to replace them. Portsmouth's reserve team had finished runners-up to Watford but could not be granted promotion, so Albion were fortunate to be re-elected to the top flight for the 1904-05 season, which they finished in mid-table. Due to financial problems the club had retained only three players. The others wanted more money and when it was not forthcoming, moved elsewhere. The standard of play deteriorated and further losses were made at the gate as the club struggled, finishing the 1905-06 season in sixteenth position.

In 1906-07, Brighton had their best season to date when they finished third in the table. This was despite pruning their playing staff from twenty one to fifteen, again because of financial problems. The club slipped down to seventeenth place the following season and in 1908-09 were eighteenth, avoiding relegation on goal average.

In 1909-10, Brighton won the Southern League First Division Championship. They lost one home game and after the turn of the year, lost one match at Southampton out of the 23 games played. The sequence included 14 wins, one of which, a 3-1 defeat of runners-up Swindon Town in the penultimate game of the season, clinched the Championship for Albion.

Home and away defeats against Swindon Town ended any hopes of the Seagulls retaining the title in 1910-11. They finished third but would have pipped Northampton Town for the runners-up spot had Brighton beaten Bristol Rovers in their last match of the season.

In 1911-12 Albion again were in contention for the Championship and beat the eventual champions Queen's Park Rangers 3-1 courtesy of a Jimmy Smith hat-trick, but had to be content with fifth place, six points adrift of Rangers. In the close season they lost a number of experienced players and ended the 1912-13 campaign in ninth place. The following season, Albion's home form kept them up with the leaders but a disappointing second-half meant a seventh place finish, eight points behind champions Swindon Town. In 1914-15 Albion finished in tenth place. When football resumed after the war, they played their last season of Southern League football prior to being admitted to the Third Division (South) of the Football League, finishing a disappointing sixteenth.

SOUTHERN PROFESSIONAL CHARITY CUP

Brighton did not enter the Southern Professional Charity Cup until 1907-08, the seventh season of the competition. After beating Queen's Park Rangers, they lost out to West Ham United in a tie that needed three matches before the Hammers went through. The following season, Albion won through to the final but lost 2-0 at home to Brentford. In 1909-10, they again reached the final after beating Reading (Home 3-1) Southampton (Home 1-0) and Swindon Town at Stamford Bridge 3-0. Their opponents in the final, also played at Stamford Bridge, were Watford and Albion won the trophy for the only time in their history with 'Bullet' Jones scoring the game's only goal.

The following season they reached the final for the third successive year but went down 1-0 to Swindon Town in the match played at Craven

Cottage. In 1911-12, Archie Needham, who had just joined the club from Wolverhampton Wanderers netted a hat-trick in a 6-2 win over Southampton before Reading ended Albion's interest in the competition.

The following season, Brighton's first round match with Southampton was drawn but because of the forthcoming FA Cup match with Everton, the club fielded the reserves in the replay. They beat the Saints 4-1 and so were retained for the rest of the competition. They went on to beat Reading and Watford before losing 4-1 after extra-time to Queen's Park Rangers in the final. In 1913-14, Albion went out at the first round stage for the first time, losing 3-0 to Croydon Common, having beaten them 5-0 in the Southern League two weeks earlier. The Seagulls last match in the competition in 1914-15 was their heaviest defeat. They went out in the first round, 5-0 at Reading.

SPEARITT, EDDIE

Eddie Spearitt was a regular in the Ipswich Town side when in January 1969, he was surprisingly allowed to leave the Suffolk club and join

Eddie Spearit
Photo: Lancashire Evening Post.

Brighton. He made his debut in a 3-1 home win over Crewe Alexandra and went on to appear in the final 18 games of the season, scoring five goals including both strikes in a 2-2 draw with Tranmere Rovers.

Over the next four seasons, Spearitt proved himself to be a versatile performer, appearing in seven different outfield shirts. By the start of the 1971-72 campaign, he had become the club's first-choice left-back and was ever-present as the Seagulls won promotion to the Second Division.

The following season, Spearitt was a model of consistency in a Brighton side that was relegated to the Third Division after finishing bottom of Division Two, and not surprisingly he was named as the club's 'Player of the Season'.

He continued his impressive displays in 1973-74 but towards the end of the season, after scoring 25 goals in 232 games, he was transferred to

Carlisle United. Injuries hampered his progress at Brunton Park and he played in only 31 games in his two seasons before moving to Gillingham where he ended his playing days.

SPONSORS

The club's current sponsors are Skint. Previous sponsors have included British Caledonian Airways, Phoenix Brewery Company, Nobo Visual Aids, TSB, Sandtex and Donatello.

STEPHENS, BERT

Left-winger Bert Stephens had been at Brentford for four years without fully establishing himself in the Bees' side when he left to join Brighton in the summer of 1935.

He made his debut in a 3-2 home win over Torquay United on the opening day of the 1935-36 season, going on to score 19 goals in 41 games as he struck up a prolific partnership with Alec Law who netted 23 goals in 32 outings. The following season Albion finished third in Division Three (South) with Stephens top scorer. His total of 24 goals included a hat-trick in a 3-0 home win over Walsall. Stephens continued to lead the way in the goal-scoring department, netting 22 in 36 games in 1937-38, including another treble in a 6-0 home rout of Exeter City. In 1938-39, Albion again finished third and Stephens was again the club's leading scorer.

During the war years, Stephens continued to turn out for Albion, scoring 68 goals in 143 games including hat-tricks against Southampton (Home 6-3 in 1940-41) Luton Town (Away 4-2 in 1943-44) and Portsmouth (Home 8-0 in 1944-45).

By the time League football resumed in 1946-47, Stephens had switched to the right-wing. He went on to score 96 goals in 205 games, a tremendous total for a winger, before hanging up his boots.

STEVENS, GARY

Although associated with Ipswich Town as a schoolboy, Gary Stevens had to go down to Brighton to begin his professional career. He made his league debut in a 2-0 home win over the Tractor Boys and then scored his

Gary Stevens
Photo: Lancashire Evening Post.

first goal for the club in the return game at Portman Road which ended all-square at 1-1.

Playing at the centre of defence alongside the experienced Steve Foster, he developed rapidly, winning his first England Under 21 cap against Hungary in April 1983 and the following month playing for the Seagulls against Manchester United in the FA Cup Final. Stevens gave a masterful performance in the exciting first match when Albion were without the suspended Foster, and managed to score one of Brighton's goals.

The south coast club were also relegated at the end of that season but Stevens, who had scored three goals in 152 games did not drop down with them, joining Spurs instead for £350,000.

He found life at White Hart Lane much harder but after being moved into midfield, he made his full international debut for England as a substitute against Finland in October 1984. After this he began to pick up a number of injuries and although he kept bouncing back, he was eventually loaned out to Portsmouth in a final effort to prove his fitness. The move was made permanent but he was still plagued by injury problems and in February 1992 was forced to retire.

STORER, STUART

After just one appearance for Mansfield Town, pacy winger Stuart Storer drifted into non-League football with VS Rugby before Birmingham City gave him the chance to resurrect his League career. At St Andrew's he became embroiled in a transfer row in a move to Everton in March 1987. He signed for the Toffees, along with Wayne Clarke, in a £300,000 deal. Wolves claimed that they were entitled to fifty per cent of any fee over £80,000 received for Clarke but Birmingham claimed he was the makeweight in the deal.

Unable to make the first team at Goodison, he joined Wigan Athletic on loan before moving to Bolton Wanderers. A regular in the Trotters' side that reached the play-offs in 1990 and 1991, he later played for Exeter City before joining Brighton and Hove Albion in March 1995.

He scored on his debut in a 3-3 draw at Birmingham City and in the following season played down both flanks for the Seagulls. A supplier of good crosses, his pace often left defenders trailing in his wake and in 1996-97 in the last game at the Goldstone Ground, scored the vital winner against Doncaster Rovers. The following season he continued to play despite a hernia problem but was eventually forced to submit to surgery. The effects of this operation, coupled with a number of minor injuries, saw his pace reduced and he ended up playing the last few of his 161 games in which he scored 14 goals at right-wing back.

Released by Micky Adams, he went into non-League football with Atherstone United.

SUBSTITUTES

The first Brighton and Hove Albion substitute was Jim Oliver who came on for Bill Cassidy against Hull City at the Goldstone Ground on 28 August 1965. The club had to wait until 16 September 1967 for their first goal-scoring substitute in the Football League when Howard Wilkinson netted in a 2-0 home win over Tranmere Rovers. A couple of weeks earlier, Paul Flood had replaced Roger Badminton in a League Cup tie against Colchester United and scored in a 4-0 win.

The greatest number of substitutes used in one season by Brighton under the single substitute role was thirty three in 1970-71. After 1986-87, two substitutes were allowed and in 1993-94, sixty one were used. Over the last few seasons, three substitutes have been allowed and 128 were used in 2000-01.

The greatest number of substitute appearances for Brighton has been made by Gerry Ryan who came on during 42 League games with ten more in cup-ties. It was in 1999-2000 that Rod Thomas rewrote the Brighton records on the matter of substitutes with an extraordinary twenty League appearances in the substitute's shirt.

One of the best substitutions occurred on 25 February 1978 when

Brighton manager, Alan Mullery, replaced full-back Gary Williams with winger Eric Potts in the match against Sunderland. The Wearsiders led 1-0 but two goals in the last three minutes from Potts gave Brighton a 2-1 win.

SUNDAY FOOTBALL

The first Sunday matches in the Football League took place on 20 January 1974 during the three-day week imposed by the government in a trial of strength with the coalminers. Albion's match against Rochdale at the Goldstone Ground was chosen as an experiment. A crowd of 18,885 – the largest of the season – saw goals from Tony Towner and Ken Beamish give Albion a 2-1 win.

SUSPENSIONS

Prior to the club's 1983 FA Cup Final, Brighton captain Steve Foster had reached 31 disciplinary points and was to be banned from the match. He decided to take his plea to the High Court but lost. In his absence, Brighton drew 2-2 with Manchester United. He came back at centre-half for the replay which Brighton lost 4-0.

T

TAYLOR, PETER

The first Peter Taylor associated with Brighton and Hove Albion found fame as Brian Clough's assistant at Derby County and Nottingham Forest. Clough always claimed they were equal managerial partners but the media did not see things this way. Whatever the secret, together they won honours galore.

Taylor began his career as a goalkeeper playing for Coventry City, Middlesbrough and Port Vale. He was managing Southern League Burton Albion when Clough asked him to join him at Hartlepool.

After moving to Derby County, they helped the Rams take the Second Division title in 1968-69, followed by the club's first League Championship in 1971-72. In October 1973 Clough and Taylor resigned their posts at Derby mainly because of the restrictions placed on Clough's media activities. The following month they had both signed five-year contracts to manage Brighton and Hove Albion.

However, the following summer, Clough negotiated a release from his Albion contract to go and manage Leeds United but Taylor stayed on as team manager. In Taylor's first season in charge, the club just avoided relegation to the Fourth Division and although they pushed hard for promotion in 1975-76, they had to settle for fourth place, three points behind promoted Millwall.

In July 1976 Taylor surprisingly resigned, rejoining his former partner Brian Clough at Nottingham Forest. They won the League Championship in 1977-78, the League Cup in 1978 and 1979 and the European Cup in 1979 and 1980. In 1981 came an acrimonious split which was never healed before Taylor's death in 1990.

TAYLOR, PETER

Rejected by Spurs as a youngster, Peter Taylor began his career with Southend United where he stood out as a player of immense potential. He was transferred to Crystal Palace, rose to Under 23 status and became one of the few Third Division players to appear in a full international for England.

Peter Taylor.

Photo: Lancashire Evening Post.

A fast raiding winger, he joined Spurs for £400,000 in September 1976 but was hampered with injuries during his time at White Hart Lane. He later moved to Orient before entering non-League football with Maidstone United. He helped out former Palace team mate Gerry Francis as a non-contract player with Exeter City before returning to Maidstone as player-manager. A member of the England semi-professional team, he managed a number of non-League clubs before taking over the reins at Southend United.

Since then he has managed Gillingham, whom he took into the First Division and Leicester City before taking charge at the Withdean Stadium last season. Taylor, who also took charge of England for their game against Italy, led the Seagulls to the Second Division Championship before parting company with the club.

TELEVISION

The Seagulls appear regularly on television nowadays and were regulars on 'Match of the Day' in their time in the First Division. Probably the first time the club appeared on the small screen was on 20 December 1958. Albion had lost 9-0 at Middlesbrough on the opening day of the season and there was much interest in the return fixture, so much so, that the game was recorded by the BBC and highlights televised during the evening. For the record, Albion lost 6-4 in a ten-goal thriller with Shepherd (2), Jones and Sexton netting for the home side.

TEMPLEMAN, JOHN

John Templeman was just 19 when he made his Brighton debut in a 2-2 home draw against Queen's Park Rangers in December 1966 and injuries apart, he kept his place for the remainder of the season. Templeman was a first team regular for seven seasons, showing his versatility by playing in seven different numbered outfield shirts. The only season he missed out on was 1969-70 when he suffered a spate of niggling injuries.

When Albion won promotion to Division Two in 1971-72, Templeman appeared in all but one League game, scoring seven goals including the club's first and last of the campaign. He also netted twice in a 5-0 win at Halifax Town and came close on a couple of occasions to completing his hat-trick. Brighton were relegated after just one season of Second Division football but Templeman remained at the Goldstone Ground for another season, taking his total of appearances in which he scored 18 goals to 255 before leaving to play for Exeter City, with Fred Binney coming in the opposite direction.

Templeman went on to appear in 200 League games for the Grecians before ending his first-class career with Swindon Town.

TENNANT, DES

Des Tennant played his early football with his home club, Cardiff City, but on being unable to make the grade at Ninian Park, drifted into non-League football with Barry Town. His impressive displays alerted a number of League clubs and in the summer of 1948, Don Welsh secured his services for Brighton and Hove Albion. Tennant made his debut at right-half in a 1-1 draw at Bristol City and, although he wore five different numbered outfield shirts, he ended his first season at the Goldstone Ground as the club's leading scorer with 10 goals.

Tennant was a virtual ever-present in the Brighton side for the next ten seasons. In 1953-54 he became the club's penalty-taker, a season in which his solid displays helped Albion finish as runners-up to Ipswich Town in the Third Division (South). Albion were runners-up again in 1955-56 before two seasons later winning the Championship with Tennant outstanding in defence.

Hampered by injuries during the latter stages of his time at Brighton, Des Tennant, who had scored 47 goals in 424 games, decided to retire.

THIRD DIVISION

Brighton have had six spells in the Third Division. The first following their admittance to the Football League in 1920-21, lasted for thirty one seasons before they won the Third Division (South) Championship in

Albion's Third Division team of 1976-77.
Photo: Lancashire Evening Post.

1957-58. In that first spell, Albion came close to gaining promotion, finishing runners-up in seasons 1953-54 and 1955-56 when only the top club were promoted but in 1947-48 they finished bottom of the Third Division and had to apply for re-election. There followed four seasons of Second Division football but relegation saw them start their second spell of Third Division football in 1962-63. It was a disastrous season as Albion were relegated to the League's basement.

Promotion two seasons later saw Albion begin their third spell in 1965-66. After seven seasons, they won promotion to Division Two as runners-up to Aston Villa but after just one season, they were back in the Third Division. After two poor seasons in which they were nearly relegated to Division Four, Albion came close in 1975-76, finishing just one place outside the three promotion-winning clubs. They gained promoted the following season as runners-up to Mansfield Town and they spent the next ten seasons playing First and Second Division football.

Albion's fifth spell in the Third Division began in 1987-88 and lasted just one season as they won promotion as runners-up to Sunderland. Although they were relegated in 1991-92, reorganisation had taken place and it was not until 1996-97 that they found themselves playing in the 'new' Third Division. Five seasons later, Albion won the Third Division Championship.

128

TOURS

Brighton embarked on their first continental tour three weeks after the end of the 1952-53 season. Their first match was in Belgium against FC Liege, the teams exchanging cuff links and tie pins before the start of the game. In an exciting match, the teams shared eight goals with Jimmy Sirrell scoring twice for the Albion. The club's second match was in the Bavarian town of Furth, Albion stepping in at the last minute after both French and Belgian teams had cancelled fixtures with the West German side. The first game in Belgium had been played under a blazing sun but the match in Germany was played in continuous rain. Despite having most of the pressure, Albion lost 1-0 with Glen Wilson putting through his own goal.

TOWNER, TONY

A good dribbler, he could play on either wing or as an inside-man. He began his career with his home-town club Brighton and Hove Albion, playing his first game for the Seagulls in a 2-0 home win over Luton Town in February 1973. He held his place in the side, playing in the last 14 games of that relegation season.

In 1974-75, Towner was the club's leading scorer with 10 goals in 41 games as Albion just avoided relegation to the Fourth Division. The following season the club just missed out on promotion but in 1976-77, with Towner scoring a number of vital goals, the club won promotion after finishing as runners-up to Mansfield Town.

The winger continued to impress and had scored 25 goals in 183 games for the Seagulls when in October 1978 he left to join Millwall. There then followed a succession of clubs – Rotherham United, Sheffield United (on loan), Wolves, Charlton Athletic, Rochdale and Cambridge United – before he played non-League football for both Gravesend and Fisher Athletic.

TRANSFERS

The club's record transfer fee received is £900,000 from Liverpool for Mark Lawrenson in August 1981. The club's record transfer fee paid is

£500,000 to Manchester United for Andy Ritchie in October 1980.

TURNER, DAVE

Dave Turner began his career with Newcastle United, helping the Magpies lift the FA Youth Cup for the first time in 1952 but found claiming a Football League place a near impossibility during his four seasons on Tyneside. After just a handful of appearances, he joined Brighton, making his debut in a 2-0 home win over Darlington.

Turner was a stalwart member of the Albion side for the next nine seasons, skippering the club in many of his 338 games in which he scored 34 goals. He helped Albion win the Fourth Division Championship in 1964-65 and was ever-present the following season as they finished their first season back in the Third Division in mid-table. He continued to be an important member of the Albion side but following a brief loan spell with Portsmouth, he left the Goldstone Ground to play for Blackburn Rovers.

He later joined Aldershot as coach, becoming assistant-manager before a ten-year stint residing in Canada.

U

UNDEFEATED

Brighton and Hove Albion have remained undefeated at home throughout just one Football League season. That was in 1964-65 when they won 18 and drew five of their games at the Goldstone Ground when winning the Fourth Division Championship.

The club's best and longest undefeated home sequence in the Football League is of 31 matches between 13 September 1975 and 20 November 1976. Brighton's longest run of undefeated Football League matches home and away is 16 between 8 October 1930 and 28 January 1931.

UNITED LEAGUE

Brighton and Hove Albion's first season in the midweek United League in 1905-06 saw them finish in seventh place out of the ten competing teams. They ended the season in fine style, beating Grays United 9-2 with both Fisher and Joynes netting hat-tricks. The following season, Albion were runners-up to Crystal Palace in the United League, losing only two of their games and drawing both meetings with Palace.

UTILITY PLAYERS

A utility player is one of those particularly gifted footballers who can play in several different positions. During Brighton's Southern League days, their best utility player was Archie Needham who joined the side from Wolverhampton Wanderers. During his time at the Goldstone Ground he played in every outfield position in the Seagulls' Southern League team.

After the mid-1960s, players were encouraged to become more adaptable and to see their roles as less stereotyped. At the same time, much less attention was paid to the implication of wearing a certain numbered shirt. Accordingly some of the more versatile players came to wear all the different numbered shirts at some stage or another, although this did not necessarily indicate an enormous variety of positions.

V

VICTORIES IN A SEASON - HIGHEST

In 1955-56, the Seagulls won 29 of their 46 league matches in finishing as runners-up in the Third Division (South).

VICTORIES IN A SEASON - LOWEST

Brighton's poorest performance was in 1972-73 when they won only eight matches out of their 42 league games and finished bottom of the Second Division.

W

WALKER, DAVE

Dave Walker played his early football with Walsall, joining Brighton in the summer of 1929. He had to wait until November of that year before making his debut at Northampton in a match Albion won 3-1, courtesy of a Hugh Vallance hat-trick. Although he scored seven goals in 14 games in 1930-31 and six goals in 15 games the following season, it was not until 1932-33 that he won a regular place in the Brighton side. After that he missed very few games in the next seven seasons, being ever-present in 1934-35.

The tough-tackling wing-half almost helped the club win promotion on a number of occasions with a best of third place in 1938-39. At the end of that season, Walker, who had been with the club for more than ten years, scoring 30 goals in 349 League and Cup games, decided to hang up his boots.

WARD, PETER

Signed from non-League Burton Albion for just £4,000, the slightly-built striker Peter Ward scored after just 50 seconds in his debut against Hereford United in March 1976. Playing in the last eight games of the 1975-76 season, he scored six goals as Albion just missed out on promotion.

Peter Ward.

In 1976-77 when Albion finished runners-up to Mansfield Town and won promotion to Division Two, Peter Ward established a new scoring record with 32 league goals. Included in this total were four goals in the 7-0 home win over Walsall. Ward's total, including cup games, was 36, a score eclipsing that of both Hugh Vallance and Arthur Attwood. He was the leading scorer in the entire Football League and was named as the club's 'Player of the Season'.

Ward led the way again the following season although he was not as prolific. His total of 17 League and Cup goals included a hat-trick in a 5-1 win over Mansfield Town. Despite a series of niggling injuries in 1978-79, he managed 13 goals in 34 games as Albion won promotion to the First Division as runners-up to Crystal Palace and reached the fifth round of the League Cup.

He was back to full fitness for the club's first season of top flight football and led the way with 18 League and Cup goals including a hat-trick in a 3-1 defeat of Wolverhampton Wanderers. During the close season he had gained a full England cap with a brief appearance as a substitute against Australia but in October 1980 he was transferred to Nottingham Forest for £400,000. After two years at the City Ground, Ward rejoined the Seagulls on loan, taking his tally of goals to 95 in 227 appearances.

WARTIME FOOTBALL

In spite of the outbreak of the First World War in 1914, the major Football Leagues embarked upon their planned programme of matches for the ensuing season and these were completed on schedule at the end of April the following year. Brighton, then in the Southern League First Division, finished in sixteenth place.

There was no competitive football in Sussex during the war but there were friendly matches between military units and various works' teams. The Goldstone Ground lay neglected for much of the First World War, and Wish Park (Aldrington Recreation Ground) was the venue for matches played by Brighton and Hove FC, a team formed to keep the best players in the district together. As things began to return to normal in 1919, the old Hove club was re-formed and took the name Brighton and Hove Amateurs to distinguish themselves from the Albion.

In complete contrast to the events of 1914, once war was declared on 3 September 1939, the Football League programme of 1939-40 was suspended and for a while there was no football. The game continued later on a regional basis and Brighton played in Football League (South 'B') and then South 'D' in the second-half of the season. Despite a number of guests turning out for Albion, there were some quite remarkable scorelines – Albion 9 Southampton 4 and Crystal Palace 10 Albion 0, being the most outrageous. Albion finished one off the bottom in South 'B' and bottom of the table in South 'D'.

In 1940-41 the Football League was split into north and south regions but because of the varying number of matches each team were expected to play, goal average was used to differentiate between teams in the table. The Christmas Day fixture at Norwich City saw the Canaries, who were strengthened by a number of Bolton players, win 18-0.

In the War Cup, Albion put up a brave fight against mighty Arsenal but lost 7-2 on aggregate over the two legs. That season, Albion beat Luton Town 7-4 with Don Welsh scoring six of the club's goals. Because of uncompleted fixtures in the Football League South, second-placed Watford objected to Brighton's claim to the title and so a challenge match was played to decide the issue and Albion won 4-1.

In 1941-42, Albion played in the London War League but despite a good start, losing only one of the opening nine matches, they ended the season in twelfth place of the sixteen competing clubs. In 1942-43, Albion competed in the South Region along with all the clubs in London and the south-east. After a poor start, their form improved and they pulled away from the foot of the table to finish twelfth of the eighteen clubs. In 1943-44, Albion held a strong Arsenal side to a 1-1 draw but won only one of their last 11 games – an 8-0 thrashing of Luton – and finished the season in sixteenth place, third from bottom.

In 1944-45, Albion made a dreadful start, losing 12 of their first 13 matches. A marked improvement in the second half of the season helped them finish fourteenth. In 1945-46 Albion competed in the Third Division (South) Southern region and finished fourth of the eleven clubs in the competition.

WEBB, CHARLIE

Charlie Webb was one of a family of seven, his father being a quartermaster in the Black Watch, serving with the British Army in Ireland. Webb joined the Essex Regiment in June 1904 and when serving in Ireland, where he was born, he played for an Irish Army XI against the English Army at Aldershot in 1907, scoring both goals in a 2-0 win.

Webb played for Ireland against England when he was with Bohemians and also represented the Irish League and Leinster. He bought himself out of the army in 1909 and after a brief spell with Worthing, joined Brighton. He made a goal scoring debut for Albion in a 1-1 draw with West Ham United, his five goals in 15 games helping the Seagulls retain their Southern League First Division status. An ever-present in 1909-10, helping Brighton to win the Southern League Championship, he was also a member of the side that beat Aston Villa 1-0 to lift the FA Charity Shield, scoring the game's only goal.

Charlie Webb.

Webb's best season in terms of goals scored was 1911-12 when he netted 17 times in 38 outings. The following season he scored four goals in the 5-2 home defeat of Southampton. Webb, who went on to score 79 goals in 280 games for Albion, saw out the last few months of the First World War as a prisoner of the Germans in the Rhineland town of Mainz and it was while he was awaiting repatriation that he was appointed as the club's manager. He managed Brighton for thirty years but was unable to get them into the Second Division, although they did go close on occasions. The Seagulls reached the fifth round of the FA Cup in 1932-33 after having to play from the first qualifying round. He was awarded a well-deserved testimonial match in September 1949 when Arsenal and Portsmouth attracted over 13,000 spectators to the Goldstone Ground.

WEBB, STAN

Goalkeeper Stan Webb played the first of his 234 League and Cup games for Brighton in a 3-1 home win over Millwall in October 1925.During his first season at the Goldstone Ground, he shared the goalkeeping duties with Walter Cook but in 1926-27 he lost out to Reg Williams, who also captained the side. With Williams an ever-present in 1927-28, it was midway through the following season before Webb won a regular place in the Albion side.

Signed from Sussex County League side Hove, when employed at the Portslade gas works, he was loaned to Tunbridge Wells Rangers during his early days with the club. In 1929-30 he missed only the final game of the season in a 4-1 defeat at Clapton Orient as Albion finished fifth in the Third Division (South). The following season he had kept 13 clean sheets in 30 games when he was injured in the 4-2 home defeat at the hands of Thames. In what was his benefit season, Webb did not play again, only returning to the side towards the end of the 1931-32 season. He was back between the posts on a regular basis during the next campaign and was the club's first-choice keeper for the next two seasons before losing his place to Charlie Thomson. Webb then joined Tunbridge Wells Rovers where he ended his first-class career.

WELSH, DON

As a player with Charlton Athletic, he had seen the London club rise from the depths of Third Division football to the top of the First Division and two FA Cup Finals in just a few seasons. As skipper of that side, Welsh had been inspirational and it was hardly surprising that someone should offer him a job in management.

He started his managerial career at Brighton and although he could not prevent the side finishing bottom of the Third Division (South) in 1947-48, his close season signings took them up to sixth place the following year.

In March 1951 Welsh was appointed manager of Liverpool and was at Anfield at a time which coincided with one of the club's lowest position in the points table. He was forced to undertake the thankless task of rebuilding but after narrowly avoiding relegation in 1952-53, there was nothing Liverpool could do to avoid the drop a year later. Although they narrowly missed out on promotion, Welsh became the first and only Liverpool manager to be sacked.

After two years running a public house in Devon, he was persuaded to take charge at Bournemouth but again had little success and was sacked during a poor 1960-61 season.

WESTERN LEAGUE

Albion gave up the United League for the Western League for the 1907-08 season, the First Division of which was played in two sections, the winners of each one playing off for the Championship. Albion finished third in the 'A' section, being unbeaten at home. In 1908-09 Albion won the Western League First Division Section 'A', finishing three points ahead of runners-up Queen's Park Rangers. Unfortunately, Millwall won the Championship play-off, beating Albion 2-1 after a 1-1 draw, with both matches played at Upton Park.

WHITING, BOB

Goalkeeper Bob Whiting joined Brighton from Chelsea in the summer of 1908. After the club's 4-1 defeat at Southampton in the third game of the 1908-09 season, Whiting made his debut at Plymouth Argyle, keeping a clean sheet in a 1-0 win. A virtual ever-present in the club's Southern League side, he helped Albion win the Western League in his first season at the Goldstone Ground.

In 1909-10, Whiting was ever-present as the club won the Southern League Championship, keeping 19 clean sheets in 42 games. When Albion beat Aston Villa 1-0 to win the FA Charity Shield, he had an outstanding game to keep the First Division club's forwards at bay.

In 1910-11, Albion almost retained their title but had to settle for third place on goal difference behind champions Swindon Town. Whiting was ever-present again in 1911-12 and kept goal in 267 matches for Brighton until the First World War. He enlisted and was killed by enemy shell-fire when tending the wounded on Vimy Ridge.

WILKINS, DEAN

Midfielder Dean Wilkins turned professional with Queen's Park Rangers but after failing to establish himself in the Loftus Road club's side, he joined Brighton and Hove Albion. He made his Seagulls' debut in a goal-less draw at Middlesbrough but after just two league appearances and a loan spell at Leyton Orient, he left the Goldstone Ground to play in the Dutch League for PEC Zwolle.

He rejoined the Seagulls in the summer of 1987 and missed only a couple of games as the club won promotion to the Second Division as runners-up to Sunderland. Thereafter he missed very few games and was ever-present in 1989-90 and 1990-91 when he skippered the club to the play-offs, only to lose to Notts County in the Wembley final.

His latter seasons with the club were plagued by injuries and at the end of the 1994-95 season, this younger brother of England international Ray Wilkins was forced to retire, having scored 28 goals in 329 games for the Seagulls.

WILKINSON, HOWARD

After joining Sheffield Wednesday as a professional in the summer of 1962, winger Howard Wilkinson found his first team opportunities limited and in July 1966, he moved to Brighton and Hove Albion.

He made his Seagulls' debut on the opening day of the 1966-67 season, scoring the club's first goal in a 2-2 draw against Swindon Town. He scored a number of spectacular goals for the Seagulls, but his main strength lay in his accurate crosses from the flank which allowed Kit Napier to score 24 goals in 1967-68 and Alex Dawson 17 in 23 games the following season. In 1969-70, his last season with the club, he switched to the left-wing as Albion finished fifth in Division Three.

Wilkinson, who had scored 19 goals in 147 games, left to manage Boston United and gained a Physical Education degree at Sheffield University. After teaching for a while he became an FA regional coach and managed England's semi-professional international team.

In July 1982 he was appointed manager of Notts County but after one season let to take charge of Sheffield Wednesday. In his first season he took the Owls back into the First Division.

He left Hillsborough in October 1988 to join Leeds United whom he took to the Second Division Championship in 1989-90. Leeds won the League Championship in 1991-92, pipping Manchester United in an exciting run-in.Wilkinson left Elland Road in 1996 and is now the FA's Technical Director.

WILKINSON, REG

Wing-half Reg Wilkinson played for both Norwich City and Sunderland before joining the Seagulls from the Roker Park club in the summer of 1924. Making his debut in a 2-0 home win over Watford midway through the 1924-25 season, he went on to give the club ten years excellent service.

His first goal came the following season in a 6-2 defeat of Aberdare Athletic as Albion finished fourth in the Third Division (South). Having missed just one game that season, he was ever-present in 1927-28 when he took over as the club's penalty-taker, scoring his first in a 2-1 reversal at the hands of Torquay United.

During the course of the 1932-33 season, in which Albion reached the fifth round of the FA Cup, Wilkinson scored the opening goal of the game against West Ham United when he lobbed the ball in off the far post. The game ended all-square at 2-2 before the Hammers won the replay 1-0.

Wilkinson went on to score 16 goals in 396 League and Cup games before hanging up his boots.

WILSON, DANNY

Northern Ireland international midfielder Danny Wilson was on the books of his home club Wigan Athletic before joining Bury in the summer of 1977. However, following the Shakers relegation to the Fourth Division, Wilson moved to Chesterfield, helping the Spireites to finish fifth in his first season at Saltergate. His impressive displays led to a transfer to Nottingham Forest but he was unable to hold down a regular place and after a loan spell with Scunthorpe United, he joined the Albion.

He scored twice on his debut as the Seagulls beat Cardiff City 3-1, going on to net 10 goals in 26 games. His midfield promptings helped Albion to finish sixth in Division Two in 1984-85 and the following season he had his best return in terms of goals, scoring 16 League and Cup goals including a hat-trick in a 5-2 League Cup win over Bradford City. However, after the club was relegated in 1986-87, Wilson, who had scored 39 goals in 155 games, left to play for Luton Town.

He netted one of the Hatters' goals in the 3-2 win over Arsenal in the 1988 League Cup Final and was the club's leading scorer in 1988-89. His next move saw him join Sheffield Wednesday, whom he helped win promotion to the top flight. He later ended his playing career with Barnsley, before becoming the Oakwell club's manager. He led the Tykes into the Premier League but lost his job after they were relegated. He then managed Sheffield Wednesday but was again sacked following the Owls' relegation. He is now manager of Bristol City.

WILSON, ERNIE

The holder of the club appearance record, Ernie 'Tug' Wilson joined Brighton from non-League Denaby United in May 1922, making the first of his 566 appearances in which he scored 71 goals in a 2-1 home win over Brentford. His impressive displays on the wing kept Brighton in the

Ernie Wilson.

hunt for promotion for a number of seasons.

An ever-present in 1924-25, he was granted a testimonial three seasons later when again he did not miss a match. Although not a prolific scorer, he did score a number of spectacular goals after cutting inside off the left flank and unleashing a powerful drive across the face of the opposition keeper. Wilson often used his speed to outpace the full-back before crossing to Arthur Attwood, Tommy Cook or Sam Jennings, all of whom benefited from having him in the side.

Wilson was granted a second benefit in May

1933 when he was given the proceeds of a match against First Division Birmingham City. His best season in terms of goals scored was 1934-35 when the popular little winger netted 11 times in 35 games. At the end of the following season, he decided to leave the Goldstone Ground, although he continued to play non-League football for Vernon Athletic in the Sussex County League for a number of years.

WILSON, GLEN

As a youngster, Glen Wilson had been on the books of his home club, Newcastle United, but it was with Brighton that he began his Football League career, making his debut in a 2-2 draw at Bournemouth in September 1949.

Over the years, he became to be known as Albion's 'Iron Man', establishing himself as one of the best wing-halves in the lower divisions. An ever-present in 1951-52 and 1953-54, he was appointed club captain midway through the decade and in 1957-58, when he missed just one game, he skippered the club to the Third Division (South) Championship.

He continued to give great service until the end of the 1959-60 season when, after scoring 28 goals in 436 League and Cup games, he left the Goldstone Ground to become player-manager of Exeter City. He had a difficult time at St James Park. The abolition of the maximum wage hitting the club hard, and it had to apply for re-election in 1960-61. Wilson had been offered the job at Exeter even though he had not applied for it, but at the end of another disappointing season, he was sacked.

WOOD, JEFF

Goalkeeper Jeff Wood began his League career with Charlton Athletic, whom he joined from non-League Harlow Town and appeared in 147 league games for the Addicks before leaving to play in Denmark. On his return to these shores he had a brief spell with Colchester United before playing for Hong Kong side Happy Valley. He later ended his league career with Exeter City.

When Steve Gritt became Brighton manager in December 1995, he took Jeff Wood as his assistant, a position he maintained when Gritt was sacked and Brian Horton appointed in his place in February 1998. A year later, Albion appointed Wood as manager until the end of the season, yet two months later he was fired.

WORST STARTS

The club's worst start to a season was in 1997-98. It took Albion nine league games to record their first victory of the campaign, drawing three and losing five of the opening fixtures. The run ended with a 2-1 success over Rochdale at the Goldstone Ground on 27 September 1997 with Mark Morris and Stuart Tuck scoring Albion's goals.

X

X

In football 'x' traditionally stands for a draw. The club record for the number of draws in a season was in 1948-49 when in finishing sixth in the Third Division (South) they drew 18 of their matches.

XMAS DAY

There was a time when Football League matches were regularly played on Christmas Day but in recent years the game's authorities have dropped the fixture from their calendar.

The last time the Seagulls played on Christmas Day was in 1957 when they drew 2-2 with Swindon Town. Brighton's first Christmas Day win was in 1911 when goals from Goodwin and Smith helped them beat Northampton Town 2-1. Their biggest Christmas Day win came in 1922 when Portsmouth were beaten 7-1.

In 1925, Eddie Fuller scored Brighton's first Christmas Day hat-trick in a 6-2 defeat of Aberdare Athletic, a feat achieved some ten years later by Alec Law as Brighton beat Bristol City 3-0.

On Christmas Day morning 1940, Brighton arrived at Norwich with only five players and despite completing a team with Norwich reserves and a few soldiers from the crowd, they were beaten 18-0, the highest margin in the history of the game involving two league clubs.

In the first two Christmas Day games after the war, the Seagulls lost 6-1 at Exeter City and 5-0 at Port Vale before recording their last Christmas Day win – a 3-0 victory at Newport County in 1952.

Y

YOUNGEST PLAYER

The youngest player to appear in a Football League game for Brighton and Hove Albion is Simon Fox who played in the Second Division match against Fulham (Home 2-0) on 23 April 1994 when he was 16 years 238 days old.

YOUTH CUP

Brighton entered a youth team in the very first FA Youth Cup competition in 1952-53, beating both Crystal Palace (Home 1-0) and Portsmouth (Away 2-1) before losing to Brentford in the fourth round. With the exception of 1957-58, Albion have always entered this competition but reaching the fourth round remains their best performance. They also achieved the feat in 1961-62, 1992-93, 1993-94 and 1999-2000.

Z

ZAMORA, BOBBY

Bobby Zamora began his career with Bristol Rovers, making his senior debut when he came from the substitute's bench in the League Cup tie against Birmingham City. After a loan spell with Bath City where he scored eight goals in six appearances, he joined Brighton and Hove Albion, again on loan in February 2000.

The young striker made a dream debut with the equalising goal in a 1-1 draw with Plymouth Argyle and then became Albion's youngest hat-trick hero when scoring three in a 7-1 win at Chester City.

In the summer of 2000 he joined the Seagulls on a permanent basis and continued where he left off on his loan spell. His tally of 31 goals in all competitions included hat-tricks in the wins over Torquay United (Home 6-2) and Macclesfield (Home 4-1). His goals were a major factor in Brighton winning the Third Division Championship in 2000-01 and, not surprisingly, he was selected for the PFA Third Division team. This stylish striker continued to score with great regularity in 2001-02, netting 32 goals in all games including another hat-trick in the 4-3 home win over Cambridge United. His goals went a long way in helping Brighton to their second successive Championship and promotion to the First Division.

Zamora, who has now scored 69 goals in 98 games for the Seagulls was selected for the England Under 21 squad participating in the European Championships in Switzerland.

ZENITH

Between 1979 and 1983, Albion sustained four seasons in Division One and came famously within a fluffed shot of beating Manchester United in the 1983 FA Cup Final.

ZENITH DATA SYSTEMS CUP

The Zenith Data Systems Cup replaced the Simod Cup for the 1989-90 season. Brighton's first match in the competition saw them well beaten 5-0 at Carrow Road by a Norwich City side. In 1990-91, the Seagulls played out a goalless draw at Plymouth Argyle before winning the tie 3-1 on a penalty shoot-out. In round two, Albion entertained Charlton Athletic, with Mike Small scoring twice in a 3-1 victory. In the quarter-final, Albion faced First Division opposition in Crystal Palace and though the game was goalless after ninety minutes, the Eagles scored twice in extra time to win the tie, but only after both of Albion's central defenders, Gary Chivers and Paul McCarthy had gone off injured.

In 1991-92, Albion beat First Division Wimbledon 3-2 with Gary Chivers scoring a last minute winner but in the southern area quarter-final, the Seagulls went out 2-0 at Upton Park to West Ham United.